Ezra Meeker: Champion

Ezra Meeker and volunteers installed his first Oregon Trail monument at Tenino on February 21, 1906. In the crowd assembled for a photograph (see page 31) that day were nearly 300 people.

ii

Ezra Meeker;
Champion
of the Oregon Trail

Includes: Hitting
the Trail in 1992

Bert and Margie Webber

WEBB
RESEARCH
GROUP
PUBLISHERS

Published by:
Webb Research Group
Books About the Oregon Country
P.O. Box 314
Medford, Oregon 97501

Library of Congress Cataloging-in-Publication Data

Webber, Bert
    Ezra Meeker, Champion of the Oregon Trail / Bert and
Margie Webber
      p.   cm.
    Includes bibliographical references and index
    ISBN 0-936738-19-7
    1. Oregon Trail. 2. Meeker, Ezra, 1830-1928. 3. Historic
sites—Oregon Trail—Conservation and restoration. I. Webber,
Margie. II. Title. III. Title: Champion of the Oregon Trail.
F880 W4 1992   92-5837
978—dc20   CIP

Contents

The Oregon Trail

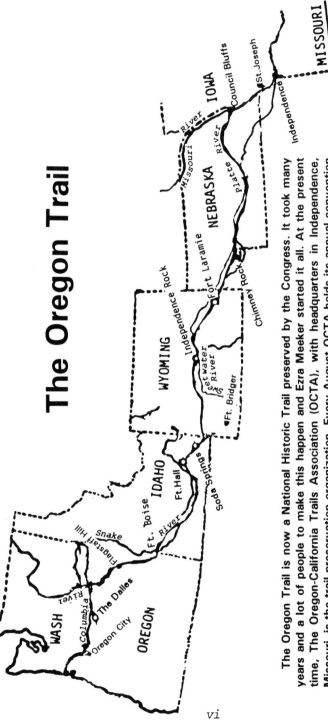

The Oregon Trail is now a National Historic Trail preserved by the Congress. It took many years and a lot of people to make this happen and Ezra Meeker started it all. At the present time, The Oregon-California Trails Association (OCTA), with headquarters in Independence, Missouri, is the trail preservation organization. Every August OCTA holds its annual convention somewhere along the trail where over one thousand trail scholars and trail buffs meet in study, listen to somewhat scholarly papers and enjoy directed field trips to nearby historical sites first written about by Ezra Meeker.

Introduction

There would be no "Oregon Trail" to enjoy today if Ezra Meeker had not set out, by himself, and without government subsidy, to preserve it.

So far as we have been able to determine, this is the first book to set forth what Ezra Meeker did, accompanied by a plethora of original and contemporary photographs, concerning his remarkable cross-country trip in 1906.

He chose to make the trip in the style of the early pioneers as a means of attracting attention and arousing enthusiasm. In both he was eminently successful.

Ezra Meeker did not attempt to make the trip alone. He had a helper and driver, Herman Goebel, who started from Puyallup with him and went as far as The Dalles. Then Meeker hired William Mardon who stayed with the long, hard pull across the country.

In addition to the 1906 trip, which was for installing monuments, he followed the Old Oregon Trail a second time in 1910 on a mission to authenticate the trail's location. In 1915 he set out again, this time in an automobile with a covered wagon top in his effort to publicize the urgent need for a transcontinental highway. It was in 1916 when he warned the government about potential trouble with Japan on the U.S. West Coast. He urged that a federally funded highway be built as a military road from coast-to-coast.

In 1924 Meeker flew over the Oregon Trail from Vancouver, Washington then all the way to Washington D.C.

Ezra Meeker wanted to have it thoroughly understood that his 1906 venture was not a money-making affair. He declared:

The expense of this expedition to perpetuate the memory of the Old Oregon Trail by erecting stone monuments is borne by myself except such voluntary aid as may be given by those taking an interest in the work, and you are respectfully solicited to contribute such sum as may be convenient."

After leaving Portland, he accepted no more contributions for the general expenses of the trip, only accepting money for monuments to be built in the places where the money was raised. Throughout this book will be found details of many of his meetings with local groups and their reactions to his proposals. In fact, a contributing reason why

20. A Typical Residence Portland, Oregon.

Portland, Oregon was the first large city Ezra Meeker visited and it was the first city in which his promotional prowess failed. Disappointed but undaunted, he moved on.

there is no Oregon Trail "Meeker Marker" in Portland can be partially laid to the public remark of a trustee of a church who would not allow the church be used by Meeker for a speech to promote his trail preservation project. The official declared that he "did not want to do anything to encourage that old man to go out on the Plains to die." Ezra Meeker left town. He was more than one hundred years too early to have known about the modern epithet which would have fit the Portland situation: "The Dogs Bark, But The Caravan Moves On!"

His personal expenses were met by his selling post card views of his outfit and some pictures of the installed monuments. A number of those photographs have been incorporated here. While he was on the road, he wrote his famous book, *The Ox Team and the Old Oregon Trail*. But it must be pointed out that during the early part of 1906 trip, Meeker and his driver Mardon, didn't eat all that well due to shortage of money. But once he had his post cards and book printed, as librarian-archivist Frank Green pointed out, "he was selling both in sufficient quantities to keep eating regularly." His book sold more than the astronomical number for the time of 34,000 copies!

Meeker, as will be found in this book, had always been a dreamer and a wheeler-dealer. The first example we see is when this 22-year-old, who was following the Old Oregon Trail in 1852, parked his wagon on the bank of the Snake River in Idaho, putting his trip on "hold," while he seized an opportunity to earn some money. He

8

started a ferry service for the benefit of caravans of pioneers coming behind him.

A few years later, Ezra Meeker, who had only wanted to be a farmer, became the largest, most influential hop grower and processor in the world. As will be pointed out here, he was the hop supplier to the famous Henry Weinhard Brewery in Portland for more than a decade.

And he had many other business interests some of which will be mentioned here. But the purpose of this book is to concentrate on his outstanding 1906 Oregon Trail preservation effort. That project, which some might think foolhardy for a man of his age—he was 76 when he started—did not slow him down. When it was over, as we will see, he just worked harder to get ready for a second trip.

Meeker was one of the best "convincers" in the nation. It can be said that he got more done toward his primary goal of Oregon Trail preservation than any other man before or since. One of his outstanding achievements was to convince the U. S. government to mint a commemorative 50¢ coin to promote his project. The coin, later

The Oregon Trail Memorial Half-Dollar

judged the most exquisite design of all U.S. commemorative coins to date, shows an ox team pulling a covered wagon on one side. But the payoff for his cause was that his Oregon Trail Memorial Association was named "sole selling agent" for the coins!

Ezra Meeker was a never-give-up type. Of course, now and then, he had some bad moments as with his rebuff in Portland, and in a few other places, but like the snap of a switch, he rebounded with seemingly endless energy.

His day-to-day progress walking across the country from his home in Puyallup, Washington to the Missouri River in 1906 is recorded here with many quotations from his original journal.

This book could never have come about without the interest and endorsement of the Ezra Meeker Historical Society, Puyallup, and specifically Mrs. Charles (Hazel) Hood, collections cataloguer of the society. Her help by locating some of the photographs and data included here was essential. We offer our sincere thanks to Mrs. Hood and to the Society.

It is important to acknowledge the friendship and professional interest in our pursuit of pertinent Meeker data by mentioning the encouragement and hands-on help given by Frank Green, recently retired librarian at the Washington State Historical Society, Tacoma. Frank had completed cataloging all of the Meeker holdings in his archives and drew from his great knowledge on the subject for our benefit. Frank Green was one of the "star players" on this venture when in its early days it was known merely as "WRG Project 19-7."

We are fortunate to have an active staff of reference librarians available to us in the Jackson County Library System's Medford, Oregon Headquarters Branch. Ann Billeter, Ph.D., directs this group of professionals who are experts in digging out answers to our most critical inquiries. We appreciate and thank all of them for their devotion and skills in the fine art of library reference work.

The authors are always open to constructive comments which should be mailed in care of the publisher at the address on page iv.

Bert and Margie Webber
Central Point, Oregon
Spring 1992

Ezra Meeker
and
volunteers
planting a
monument

Chapter 1
The Young Ezra

Ezra Meeker always wanted to be a farmer. While he was courting the girl on the neighboring farm in his 21st year, she received his ideas with enthusiasm. The two made a pact to become farmers and some day to own their own land. It came to be.

Young Meeker was a possibility thinker and was never known to let any grass grow under his feet. In time, in the Puyallup Valley of Washington, he became the "hop king" of the world. His farming was a great achievement to the betterment of the hop industry as well as to his adopted State of Washington—he had arrived in pre-territorial days—and to himself. He would write many books. One, in 1883, was the greatest treatise on hop growing and hop handling published to that time.

Ezra Meeker, a son of Jacob Redding Meeker and his wife Phoebe (Baker) Meeker, was born near Huntsville, Butler County, Ohio on December 29, 1830. His earliest home was in a log cabin.

At the age of 5, young Ezra was sent to a local school master for his beginning education. This venture was short lived when on the youngster's failure to respond to the teacher's demand for a specific recitation, the boy was up-ended onto the teacher's lap for a spanking. And Ezra bit him! This incident ended the boy's education for the time being.

Of the several sources checked on Meeker's early days, there are variances in days, periods of times and distances between points. One reference claims when he was about 7, the family moved by ox team to Covington, Indiana. The next move was to a point west of Indianapolis where his father worked in Carlyle's Flouring Mill. Apparently Ezra was entered in a school again but his piecemeal autobiography claims this was in Lockland, Ohio but he does not give a date. About his schooling, he wrote:

> I played hooky instead of going to school but one day while under the canal bridge, the noise of passing teams so freightened me that I ran home and betrayed myself. Did my mother whip me? Why, God bless her dear old soul—no. Whipping children, though, both at home and in the school room was then about as common as eating one's breakfast; but my parents did not think it was necessary to rule by the rod, though then their family government was exceptional.

Young Meeker was always restless. His parents recognized this and did not insist on schooling. Ezra was able to work on the family farm where his help was dearly needed as times were always hard. Everyone worked long hours and accepted responsibilities. His brother, Oliver, was two years older.

About the neighbor girl, Eliza Jane Summer, the two young people got along fine and decided to marry. Eliza Jane was 17. Ezra lauded his wife by writing:

> [She] could sew and she could weave, make delicious butter, knit soft, good-shapen socks, and cook a meal as any other country girl around about, and withal as buxom a lass as had ever been born and raised [in Indiana].

Ezra proposed a move away from the two families' places about the time of the marriage and found no objection when be announced, "We will go west and not live on pap's farm. Nor in the old cabin nor in any cabin unless it is our own." Eliza Jane reportedly responded in the affirmative.

*   *   *

The first week of October 1851 was of great importance for the young people. They married then moved away.

They packed their belongings into a covered wagon and headed into Iowa. The young couple planned as carefully as possible. They loaded "a good old-fashioned feather bed, a good size Dutch oven and each an extra pair of shoes." There was cloth enough for Eliza Jane to make two dresses and a pair of pants for her husband. For food, the teenage bride packed "cake, apple butter and pumpkin pies, jellies...enough to last the whole trip [about 500 miles] and then some."

The couple left in high spirits spurred on with the good wishes from parents and friends. They were leaving in delightful Indian summer weather. Ezra had a few dollars in his pocket, a minimum of belongings and great confidence in their future. The couple were each in good health. They had each other and they were very happy.

Ezra and Eliza Jane were greeted at their destination by the onset of a winter that was to be one of the coldest, meanest, Iowa winters of record. Ezra took a job as a cook in a surveyor's camp but the cold was too much for him so be became a flag man. He decided Iowa winters were not for him. Men in the camp were talking of going to the Oregon country and with Ezra's seemingly built-in restlessness, it didn't take much chatter before he was eager to try his hand in Oregon. Besides, he learned, government land was free to homesteaders in Oregon and if he stayed in Iowa, we would have to pay for any land. It didn't take any special encouragement for Eliza Jane to agree to a move west for she too was complaining of the cruel Iowa winter.

But there were challenges. Oregon was a "foreign" land. If they went they would be "emigrants," for the Oregon country was well beyond the limits of the then United States. They would have to carry basic furnishings with which to set up housekeeping there. It would be necessary to plan carefully for they would also have to pack essential foods to be used all along the way and it would be a very long, tedious trip. Ezra took his planning seriously and in his usual stride.

He considered their recent successful trip to Iowa from Indiana as a shakedown adventure for his big move to Oregon. Thus were his dreams. But an actual decision about making such a wonderful and exciting trip had to be put off for two reasons. It was still winter and trips to Oregon could not leave until spring. Also, Eliza Jane's first pregnancy was advancing. They could plan, but they would have to wait on the circumstances in which they found themselves.

Ezra and Eliza Jane's first born, a son, whom they named Marion, came into the world in March 1852. About one month later, the couple believed all was well therefore they announced plans for their overland trip to the Oregon Country for that year.

But one slight matter Eliza, in her packing, had not been aware: In the hot sunny days, her butter, packed in the flour, melted. Was this a disaster? Undaunted, Eliza Jane made short-cake. Were they then short of butter? Not hardly, for the constant jostling of the wagon automatically churned fresh butter from the cream off the daily milking, which had been placed in a can in the wagon. And there were plus values: whipping cream and buttermilk!

Keeping in mind that their journey started in the spring, and wild strawberries were easily found, did Eliza Jane treat her husband to fresh strawberry shortcake and whipped cream? Ezra didn't mention strawberries when he recalled:

> What a luxury, yes, that's the word—a real luxury! I will never, so long as I live, forget that short[bread] and corn bread, the puddings and pumpkin pies [but] above all, the buttermilk. It is the small things which make up the happiness of life.

Ezra Meeker did not join any organized company or caravan but he did not want to travel alone. When first getting started, he met several men and with gentlemanly agreement, they decided to travel together. (This group was composed of four wagons and nine men, including Ezra's brother Oliver, two McAuley sisters, plus Eliza Jane and the baby. The group proved congenial. Each had his own supplies but there was some sharing. They crossed most of the country together and separated only as some left for California when they reached a parting place in Idaho.)

Ezra, young and idealistic, began to have realizations of the great risks one took by setting out on a 2,000 mile months-long trip toward the land beyond the sunset. They passed parties parked aside the trail with some member desperately ill. They also met and talked with people going the other way—east. These were the "go-backs." People who, for their own reasons, gave up along the way and turned around.

Young Meeker learned there were many reasons why people gave up their dreams of living in the Oregon Country Some just changed their minds. Others had severe equipment breakdown and turned back while they were still "early" on the trek. But many were going home without a son, a daughter, a wife, and some women with children had lost their men. Dreaded cholera, was a part of it. And cholera seemed to be everywhere.

As it turned out, Ezra was glad that Eliza Jane insisted on clean hands before sitting down to eat.

Chapter 2
Planning the Long Trip to Oregon

Years later, Ezra wrote about the trip in some detail starting with outfitting:

> I have been asked hundreds of times how many wagons were in the train I traveled with, and what train it was, and who was the Captain, assuming that of course we must be with some train. When we drove out of Eddyville, there was but one wagon in our train, two yoke of four-year-old steers, one yoke of cows, and one extra cow. This cow was the only animal we lost on the whole trip—strayed in the Missouri River bottom before crossing.
>
> William Buck, who became my partner for the trip, was a man six years my senior, had had some experience on the plains and knew well as to an outfit needed, but [he] had no knowledge as to a team of cattle. He was an impulsive man and to some extent excitable, yet withal a man of excellent judgment and honest. He was scrupulously clean. His aptitude for camp work and unfitness for team handling easily divided the chores.

This was a strange arrangement with the bachelor in camp while the married man and father would be out driving the team and handling the extra cattle.

Crossing Iowa, they struck up an acquaintanceship with Thomas McAuley. He had a cool, self-assured manner and was heading for California. They decided to travel together until the McAuleys branched off to their destination.

Eliza Jane, whom Ezra would remind us in his many writings was of robust health, had responsibility for the baby as well as for domestic chores. These would include all the cooking, a task she enjoyed even under day-to-day intransit situations, and doing the washing when there was a place or a time to do it—a chore she did not enjoy. But Eliza was a tidy person and wanted her man to look good even on the dusty trail.

Bill Buck chose goods needed for the trip to be hauled in the wagon while Ezra shopped for a team. Eliza Jane made butter which she packed in the center of the flour which had been double-sacked for protection. She put eggs, well separated so they would not break, in the corn meal. Her plan for carrying food was to have enough "perishables" to last for about 500 miles. They packed every kind of fruit they could obtain—mostly dried—including pumpkins. They also took beef jerky "but not too salty." Eliza had put together home-made yeast cakes thus they enjoyed light bread all along the 2,000 miles to the Oregon Country. She did this baking in a small tin reflector instead of in a heavy Dutch oven that was considered the usual method.

Chapter 3
The Trip Starts

The trail was clogged with emigrants to the extent that in some places wagons often traveled several abreast. As the days wore on, Ezra counted more than 50 graves less than one week old. Accidents accounted for some deaths but cholera was the real killer.

All of these deaths made a great impression on the young man to the extent that years later, when he considered measures to preserve the Oregon Trail, he envisioned permanent, granite markers which would not just mark the trail, but be memorials to all those who died along the way to Oregon.

Each day, one of the men moved ahead of the party to look for a camping place. Being the scout was not an easy job and could never be taken lightly. A suitable site would include good grass, water and firewood as well as a location that would more-or-less comfortably handle the number of wagons and people in the caravan. As the numbers of emigrants and their animals increased, it was not uncommon for the grazing land to be several miles away from the trail. Good water was difficult to find. Little wells yielded brackish water. McAuley urged that the group take their water from the river. Each wagon had some buckets or small barrels in which a day's supply of water was carried.*

The little wagon caravan was unique in that no person was elected captain. McAuley was the oldest and to him fell the task of train organization and direction. Ezra was the only married man in the group. He was also the youngest. Because he was strong and was young, many of the heavy chores fell to him. He started the trip somewhat overweight, but by the time he arrived in Oregon, any flabbiness was gone.

Perhaps the most courageous member of the entire party was Eliza Jane Meeker. By now she was 20 with babe-in-arms. She stood ready to shoulder her share of the responsibilities. Regrettably, the robust health she started with did not last the trip. But her courage never failed.

Chapter 4
Miles of Covered Wagons

The army of emigrants, stretching in a near-unbroken line for about 500 miles seemed obsessed with the idea of haste. Almost everyone wanted to move right along as if the land in Oregon was limited.

The mania for speed was such that many emigrants lightened their loads by casting off essential goods along the way. Many, who had brought spare wagons, left them behind.

It had been determined in the earlier years of travel over the emigrant trail, that Indians sometimes swooped down on single or small groups of wagons but left the long, continuous trains alone.

Indians were "gatherers." If someone on the trail left something out in the open be it a piece of clothing or an animal, watchful Indians often "gathered" these items which they then called their own. The emigrants called this "stealing" therefore these incidents sometimes

---

*In all of the diaries and other books about the Oregon Trail the authors have perused, never have they read where any of the pioneers boiled the water before drinking it.

led to killings on both sides. At night it was necessary for at least one man in the group to stay awake to be on guard against Indian "gatherers."

Days and days passed with slow, methodical progress being made. All the while from the Missouri River, the trek had been uphill toward the summit of the Rocky Mountains. But the grade was slight and for the most part was not realized for hundreds of miles. Even so, there were summer thunderstorms that crashed upon the pioneers wetting everything they owned. And there was dust. In the large trains, a roster of rotation of wagons was kept to make certain every wagon had a chance to be in front where there was no dust.

Jane Gould, traveling on the trail in 1865, would tell her diary:

> The dust is even worse than Indians,
>   Storms,
> Or winds, or mosquitoes,
>   Or even wood ticks!
> Dust....
>   If I could just have a bath!*

Past Fort Laramie, the nights grew colder and often on awakening in the morning, there would be thin ice on the top of the water buckets. The route from the Missouri River had been uphill but the climb was almost unnoticeable until reaching the great South Pass at 7,500 feet elevation. After leaving Pacific Springs, the sharp descent began. .

The trail did not seem so crowded now and not nearly as dusty. But more than half the journey was still before them. Teams of animals, wagons and people all move faster going down hill therefore every one was in better spirits.

In Idaho, those going to California branched to the southwest. Those for Oregon kept straight ahead. When Ezra reached the Snake River he had to make a choice. They could follow the rim of the canyon where grazing was limited or they could risk a crossing where there was good feed. The latter was the decision. Ezra and Eliza emptied all of their belongings from the wagon then Ezra upended the wagon and caulked the seams to make a waterproof boat. With their possessions again loaded, they slowly crossed the Snake River to its north bank.

Young Ezra would become one of the world's best promoters and

*Quoted from *The Oregon & California Trail Diary of Jane Gould in 1862. See:* bibliography

now, on the Snake River in 1852, he launched that career. A second crossing of the river was indicated by the guide book about 150 miles ahead. This was about a ten day journey by wagon, but Ezra thought he would go it alone in three. He considered and acted on an idea to establish a ferry business. He and his brother left at once. When his party reached the crossing, they found him and Oliver, and some others engaged in a lucrative ferry business. They had lashed two wagons together to form a suitable floating platform for the transport of people and goods. The Meeker party camped here for a number of days while the boys made money. Finally, the young brothers sold their interests for $180 and returned to the trail.

This was just the first of Ezra's "deals." In the action packed years to follow, he would be many things including an innkeeper, longshoreman, merchant, farmer, "hop king", banker, politician, miner, author of books and lecturer. Of all these interests, Ezra's ability as a promoter never wavered.

The end of the overland portion of their journey was near at hand. After they ascended the rugged and dangerous Burnt River Canyon in Oregon they came out on the bluff at Flagstaff Hill that looked out across what was then called The Lone Pine Valley. This was the Powder River Valley in Baker County. Across this lush green valley lay another 4,000 foot barrier, the Blue Mountains. Finally, on the western down-hill side of the Blues, they eventually came to The Dalles, the place on the Columbia River where a major decision had to be made.

From The Dalles, the pioneers could continue by wagon over the dangerously steep Barlow Toll Road which passed over the southeast shoulder of Mt. Hood to Oregon City, or they could leave their wagons and take boats down the river. The Meeker family decided to put all their belongings on a scow then they floated down the Columbia River to the cascades where they put ashore. Below the falls, they took passage on a steamer the rest of their way to Portland. Had Ezra not become engaged in the ferry business back in Idaho, he would not have had the cash for the fare on the boat. As it was, they landed in Portland with just $3.75 in hand. Here Ezra and Oliver split their wealth. Oliver accepted $1.75 and Ezra, with a baby and a very sick wife, got $2.00.

18

Claimed to be the first picture taken on Front Street in Portland, 1852. Note mast of ship, left, rear, the ship tied up in the Willamette River.

Chapter 5
Getting Started in the Oregon Country

Portland was a city of tents, a few shacks, stumps and a lot of mud for it was raining. It was the first of October and it was a dismal day.

Eliza Jane was not well. Ezra found lodging in a flimsy lodging house where she could rest. Rent for a few days took the rest of his money. He found a job as a longshoreman unloading a ship. The work was hard and the hours were long but the couple needed the money and a job was a job. Word came from Oliver, who had gone on ahead, for them to come to St. Helens where a boarding house proposition awaited him. At least that would provide a roof over their heads. Although the work unloading the ship had been backbreaking, Ezra had earned the large sum of $40.

A dock was under construction at St. Helens where about sixty men were employed. Oliver had rented a house where these men could be lodged and boarded. Accordingly, the Meekers did a brisk business until a day when word arrived that the steamship company that needed the dock decided to pull out. While this put the Meekers out-of-business, it brought Ezra and Eliza Jane to the recollection that they had come to Oregon to farm.

His first so-called farm home was a log cabin Ezra and Oliver put up on a claim at what became Kalama in Washington. Luckily, the site was a distance away from the banks of the river for the Columbia River rose that winter in a flood. As a result, perfectly good saw logs that floated down river were left piled along the banks as the water receded. Ezra was not a man to pass up a good profit so he gathered the logs, cut more from a nearby stand of trees then sold them to a mill.

By early spring, Ezra was planting crops but he did not have a feeling of being settled. When word was received that a new Territory was to be carved out of Oregon, he was interested. Eliza Jane was not pleased to learn they would be moving again but she was resigned to it when Ezra and Oliver, with packs on their backs, set out on an exploring mission.

At what became Olympia, a village of about 100 people, they were not impressed with their first view of Puget Sound for all they saw was mud flats because the tide was out. But they built a flatboat and shoved off. They eventually came opposite the Puyallup Valley and with an Indian guide, explored part of it but passed it by because it was so full of huge trees it was no place for farmers who needed clear land.

The pair continued their exploration but turned back to the Steilacoom area because of the development they had seen there. They realized if they went into farming near by, its produce would sell well.

Ezra and Oliver located a claim on the east side of McNeil Island facing Steilacoom. While Ezra returned to get Eliza Jane and Marion at the cabin on the Columbia River, Oliver was to build a house on the island.

On his return with his family, Ezra expressed delight with the setting. Looking out of the single, glass window in their new home, he could see the bay in the foreground, a budding city on the shore and the greatness of ever present snow-capped Mount Rainier looming on the horizon.

A series of events followed. A letter brought news that Ezra's parents wanted to come to Oregon and asked if Oliver could return to them in Indiana and help with the trip. This was arranged and Oliver left. In the summer of 1854, word came that the wagon train was in trouble so Ezra, once again leaving his family, set out to help. He went over Naches Pass, a rough road through the Cascade Mountains, but it was a significant short cut. He found the overland caravan near old Fort Walla Walla and was disheartened to learn his mother and younger brother had died on the trail. He led the remaining members of the family back over the Naches Trail to his place at McNeil

Island.

It was decided the island claim had many limitations so the enhanced family took a claim under the Oregon Land Act southeast of Tacoma. They built another house and decided to farm, as well as operate a general store in Steilacoom which they called J. R. Meeker & Sons. But being a businessman was not Ezra's ambition and fate stepped in that brought disaster to the family and to the enterprise. Oliver had been sent to San Francisco as a buyer for the store. On his return on the ship *Northerner,* the ship sank off the California coast on January 5, 1861 and Oliver drowned.

In the meantime, Ezra was exploring the Puyallup Valley, the place of the huge, tall trees they had dismissed earlier, because he learned that excellent vegetables could be grown there. In time, he bought out a claim and once again moved his family—now four children—to the Puyallup Valley. He arrived broke. He did not have even a coat on his back. But he did own one oxen, seven cows and some chickens. Ezra was still the possibility thinker and would not give up. He planted farm produce and he planted hops. (For years he was the hop supplier to Portland brewer Henry Weinhard.) In a few years be became the Hop King of the world as well as the wealthiest man in the state and a promoter for Western Washington.

Ezra Meeker was an active man. He was a member of groups that among other projects fought for better roads, schools and helped form a public library. But he was a farmer and a promoter at heart. He platted and founded the town of Puyallup in 1877. His first home site in the valley is marked today with an ivy covered pergola in Pioneer Park.

In 1877 work started on the Meeker Mansion, one of the largest and most expensive homes in Pierce County. It rose to three stories and had 17 rooms. It is today the home of the Ezra Meeker Historical Society, Inc., a non-profit educational corporation.

Chapter 6
The Entrepreneur

The hop farms and the hop business came to a disastrous end when the crop was viciously attacked and destroyed by aphids. There was thought that the barrier of the Cascade Mountains and its icy winters would prevent the insect invasion and although the crop had been successful for many years, the end came without notice.

Ezra Meeker employed every eradication means possible but he could not get ahead of the little pests. His hop business, and that of his hop-growing neighbors, was literally eaten by the insects. In almost no time at all, he was out of business and nearly out of money.

He became president of a bank (but only for a very short time) by default, when the officers moved out of town sometime between sundown and the next sunrise on a given day. Meeker didn't know it, but the bank was about to go broke. It was not a happy time. With his own money, raised by pledging his land, he arranged to pay all the depositors even getting them out of bed at night before bank examiners arrived the next morning.

There had been a lot of news in the papers about the gold strike in the Yukon. Although Ezra was determined not to set off for a gold mining experience, he was certain, even at age 68, there must be some way he could find a profitable venture in the frozen north. He had a lot of imagination and he put it to work.

From the garden, he had tons of vegetables. He and Eliza Jane spent most of the winter drying and canning them. In the spring of 1898, he, a son-in-law Roderick McDonald, and his son Fred, and others, started for Alaska burdened with all those canned vegetables. In addition, he took crates of 500 live, cackling chickens.

Arriving in Dawson, they set up shop and quickly sold everything they had. Still looking for a good deal, Ezra Meeker invested $19,000 profit from the food business in a gold mine and quickly lost his shirt. He returned to Puyallup broke, where he spent his time writing books. He also became President of the Washington State Historical Society.

For many years Ezra Meeker had cherished the idea of preserving the grand old Oregon Trail. It was that trail that had primarily populated Oregon and Washington and provided thousands more who turned off to California after gold was discovered there, at Sutter's Mill, by two visiting Oregonians.

Meeker, a great promoter, envisioned permanent, granite monuments along the trail. Such markers would perpetuate the memory of the trail and honor the thousands who started, but died along the way.

Ezra Meeker in his "later" years— sometime after 1906—but we do not know when the picture was made.

Chapter 7
Planning the Grand Adventure

Ezra Meeker spent several years writing, lecturing, and brain-storming how he would handle his grand scheme for marking the Old Oregon Trail. His first realization was that if he, or anyone else for that matter, was to place markers along the trail, he would have to get on with it without delay. This was because the old trail was being plowed up by farmers a little at a time. And towns and cities had been growing at locations along the trail and often, now, the trail was being buried under streets and buildings. For these prime reasons, Meeker considered any delays would be costly to his trail preservation plan. Time was of the essence.

He realized that such a trip would in itself take a lot of time for he wanted to present to the people what it was truly like to travel the trail in a covered wagon pulled by oxen as he had done back in 1852. He would have to engage in showmanship to get the point across. He would have to actually show them. He was certain his arrival in towns and cities along the way in a covered wagon would arouse at first curiosity, then keen interest as he explained his trail preservation plan. He was certain that newspapermen would follow him because his story would be different—even odd. He would be a publicity seeker for a good cause, he believed. And once on the trail, he assured himself, the newspapers would provide dozens of feature stories that would arouse the population to underwrite his trail marking plan. Meeker's promotional fires were burning within him and would carry his program to undreamed of heights.

But all this would be costly even for 1906. Meeker was a comparatively poor man. His fortune in the hop business had been lost. But enthusiasm burned within him and his old resourcefulness came to the fore once again. From friends he obtained money to get started.

Ezra set to the task of locating a yoke of oxen and a suitable wagon. But a span of oxen would be hard to find for automobiles were becoming common and crude trucks were now providing limited hauling services. The railroads were the major cross-country form of transport. The primitive ox was becoming something of a rarity.

Finally a yoke of oxen was found but one was unsuitable for such a

The Meeker Mansion in Puyallup as it appeared in 1906 when Ezra Meeker used his front yard for a shake-down camping experience just before hiting the trail.

lengthy venture. Nevertheless, the owner insisted if Meeker wanted the good animal, he would have to buy both of them. The good ox was named "Twist" and hauled to the Tacoma stockyard where Meeker had arranged to keep him until leaving time. The chance of obtaining a second ox was minimal so when a herd of Montana steers arrived, Meeker inspected each carefully seeking one that be could team with Twist. He said one of the animals had a kindly eye and was of the correct height to be a team-mate for the ox and of course, as a five-year-old, was physically strong. This steer he named "Dave."

Ezra Meeker's "Dave" would draw the covered wagon 9,000 miles, gain 860 pounds under yoke and was destined to become America's most famous steer.

But these animals, total strangers to each other, were hard to break into wearing a yoke. Eventually, the animals, having no choice in the matter, settled down and Ezra started for Puyallup. It was a rough trip—sort of on-the-job training—as these animals had to learn a "Hee" from a "Haw" and how to respond to reins. By the time Meeker got the pair to his home, they, and he, were exhausted. Dave, the steer. really didn't want anything to do with Ezra so it took several days for Dave settle in.

In the meantime, Meeker had been searching for an authentic covered wagon. To his chagrin, none could be found. But he did locate

25

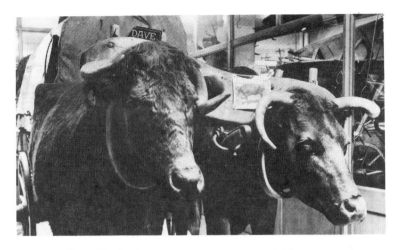

Ezra Meeker's famous ox team, and his wagon, has been preserved and is exhibited in the Washington State Historical Society's Museum in Tacoma.

a lot of parts. He found a wheel hub from a wagon that crossed the country in 1853. From two other antiques he salvaged hub bands, braces, boxes, and other fittings, including a tar bucket that some claim was over 100 years old.

All his parts were delivered to Cline & McCoy who operated a shop at what is now 204 East Pioneer Avenue in Puyallup. Here the firm built a sturdy wagon with wooden axles, linch pins and steel skeins. So well was the job done, that the extent of repairs needed along the road that out-of-pocket costs were limited to 50 cents!

As pointed out, friends provided funds for Meeker to get his rig and animals together. Charles Hood was the proprietor of the largest hardware store in the Puyallup Valley. For years he had been storing an old yoke against a time he might need it. Now was that time. Charley Hood gave the yoke as well as special shoes for the team to Ezra. (One-piece horse shoes would not properly fit Twist and Dave because their hooves, not at all similar to those of horses, are cloven—divided into two parts.)

And Ezra knew that people loved dogs so he sought to obtain a suitable, fairly large but friendly dog not only as a companion, but as part of his traveling exhibit.

Ezra Meeker knew full well his venture would have challenges for there was competition out there. Common to the era were traveling salesmen in wagons. These men put on entertainment to get attention to their various products which included everything from pots and pans to patent medicine. These were the "snake-oil" hucksters.

26

"Jim" was a Scotch Collie, and served as a watch dog as well as being a faithful companion on the trip. The dog and the oxen did not get along.

But Meeker's approach would be different. He would appear in a genuine covered wagon reminiscent of the ones used on the Old Oregon Trail. Further, Ezra wore a full beard, and in his senior-citizen age, 76, the tales he would tell of his trail experience of 1852 would be genuine. Many people he would meet had arrived in wagons just like his and would be vividly reminded of their own trail experience. He looked and acted the part. He was real.

To pay for the granite markers he wanted to place along the trail, he would depend on his ability to lecture about his burning desire to preserve the Old Oregon Trail. He believed this would win the support of the people. On his plea for money he needed tro have the people with him therefore he did not want to be extravagant. He would ask only for pennies and nickels with which to buy monuments to mark and save the trail for the children. He always tried his best to get children into his plans. He was convinced he would be successful. He believed that prosperous business people would contribute much. But he was most firm that his public promotion would be for "pennies and nickels."*

*People who gave large sums did so because they believed in Meeker's project as there was no "tax write-off" incentive at that time. The Federal income tax for businesses was not enacted until 1909. For indivividuals, there was no "cheritable contribiution" deduction against personal income as there was no personal income tax until 1913.

5. *Shoeing the Oxen, Seattle, 1906.*

The post cards Meeker sold included scenes along the trail as well as pictures of preparations and maintenance. The oxen are being shod (top) in Seattle before the trip. The job had to be done again (lower) at The Dalles.

Ezra needed to hire a driver. And there would be personal costs along the way. He reasoned once the people knew what he was doing, they would supply the money. *

There were detractors from the start. He would assemble his team and go about the Puyallup Valley on shakedown day trips. Some people along the way, remembering Meeker as the world famous and moneyed Hop King, and employer of over 1,000 persons in his hop processing business, now openly made fun of him—a bedraggled old, bearded man who, now in his seventies— was planning on walking across the nation on a personal whim to promote the preservation of the Old Oregon Trail. To the teen-agers he met in Puyallup, this was unbelievable. Some of his relatives tried to talk him out of it. But Meeker was resolute and fully determined to carry out his mission.

His first full dress rehearsal was called "Camp No. 1" and was in the front yard of his mansion. Here well-wishers and detractors too came to venture a look at what some must have called a spectacle.

The old man had his tent pitched on the grass with his wagon and team-in-yoke standing to the side. Meeker was dressed in a wrinkled, baggy gray suit with the tops of his pants stuffed inside his well-made, sturdy boots. His mop of gray whiskers hid a necktie, if he was wearing one. He had a hat perched on his head from under which protruded tufts of white hair. On his nose and hooked to his ears was a pair of thin, goldrimmed spectacles.

Ezra Meeker was ready. Would he and his mission be accepted?

---

*Meeker would take pictures along the way as well as write a book about his 1906 trail experience while on the trail. He would do the writing during "nooning" and sometimes at night. When he got to Lincoln, he contracted with a printer to make the book so he would have it to sell as he continued his promotional travel in the Eastern United States. Meeker had a plan and he worked it well.

Ezra Meeker's expedition followed many miles of old Oregon Trail ruts.

Chapter 8
Hitting the Trail in 1906

Ezra Meeker's Camp No. 1 was maintained for several days to observe all of its physical aspects and to make changes before getting underway.

Meeker's Camp No. 2 was set up merely six blocks from his starting place. He pitched his tent and tethered his team in the street in front of the Methodist Church. Inside the building that night, he delivered a major speech on the need to preserve the Old Oregon Trail making certain his neighbors understood his mission. He also let them know donations were acceptable and expected.

Between Puyallup and Olympia he made additional overnight stops as continued "shakedown" and to talk with people as they came by curious as to what this strange outfit and its elderly, bearded gentlemen was doing. He finally got under way from Camp No. 9 at Olympia on February 19, 1906. He went as far as Tumwater, 2 miles, where he set a post to be subsequently replaced with a permanent stone marker

At Tenino, the citizens had already prepared a suitable stone and on February 21, a ceremony of dedication was held where nearly the

Ezra Meeker's first triumph with monument installation was at Tenino, Washinton where nearly all of the town turned out. Lower picture made in 1987. See the *Frontispiece*.

entire population of the town turned out.*

At Centralia, contributions were sufficient enough to warrant ordering a stone, properly inscribed, which was later positioned on the road a short way out of town.

In Chehalis, a place was selected in the park (Court House lawn) with a post being set where an inscribed monument would stand. This was undertaken by the town's Commercial Club, which today would probably be called the Chamber of Commerce.

Three miles southwest of Chehalis is the former village of

---

*The official western terminal of the Oregon Trail is recognized as Oregon City. In Meeker's enthusiasm, he installed monuments at other places plausibly in exchange for public support for his program. As to a so-called "official list" of Meeker trail markers, *see:* Appendix.

Claquato on the Skookumchuck River. Meeker noted that Louis H. Davis, the founder, "provided $50 to erect a monument and $50 for the purchase of one ox for the expedition.

Jackson is a state historical site about nine miles south of Chehalis. It was here in 1845 where the first home in western Washington was built by John R. Jackson, the building also serving for the first session of the Lewis County Court in October 1851. When Ezra Meeker proposed a trail marker here, one of Jackson's daughters, Mrs. Ware, and her husband, indicated the spot where the monument should be erected so a post was planted. Mrs. Ware placed the post in place while her husband tamped the earth around it. A stone was ordered at once to replace the post.

The village of Toledo on the Cowlitz River was to receive a monument to be paid for by the town. The marker was to replace a post set by Meeker.

In Portland, on March 2, he was permitted to set up his camp on the property of Jacob Kamm where he remained until March 9. He was in town, in his words, "to test the question of securing aid for the expedition." Nearly everyone took a lively interest in the "novel undertaking" and his "unique outfit" yet it was very plain that only a few believed the project could be successfully carried out by an individual. The prevailing comments were that this venture should be government sponsored and funded.

Crossing the Burnt River in Eastern Oregon. Jim out in front.

At The Dalles, large, enthusiastic crowd greeting him.

Chapter 9
Meeker's Achievements in Oregon

In Portland, a trustee of a large church voted against Meeker's use of the church for a lecture about the expedition saying he "did not want to do anything to encourage that old man to go out on the plains and die." But through the efforts of George H. Himes of the Oregon Pioneer Association (later to be come the Oregon Historical Society), an influential gentlemen, nearly $200 was contributed. (There is no record of a Meeker monument being installed in Portland.)

On March 10, Meeker had his outfit loaded aboard the steamer *Baily Gatzert* for the trip up the Columbia River to The Dalles. On debarking, he was greeted by a large, enthusiastic crowd that conducted him to a place they had selected for his camp. Meeker had written earlier to a landmark committee asking for cooperation to secure funds to erect a monument. The suggestion saw immediate action for when he arrived, a monument was already in place and merely awaited his dedication speech. Alas, the fierce cold wind, for which The Dalles is a regular recipient, spoiled the plans and the dedication was put over until the 12th. Meeker stayed in town until the afternoon of the 14th declaring:

I have always felt that here was the real starting point as from here there would be no more shipping [the outfit] but all driving. By rail it is 1,734 miles from The Dalles to Omaha where our work on the old Trail ends. By wagon road the distance is probably 1,800 miles. The load was heavy. With a team

After he arrived in Pendleton, Meeker bought a "kodak" which, during that era, was the universal word for any kind of camera. The crowd for the dedication of the monument was over 1,000.

untrained on the road and one ox unbroken and no experienced ox driver and the grades heavy, small wonder if a feeling of depression crept over me. The unbroken ox, on heavy grades, would move [ahead] one or two wagon lengths at a time and on level roads in warm sun, would poke out his tongue. He was like a young sprig out of school with muscles soft and short breath.

It took fourteen days to drive to Pendleton, a distance of 138½ miles, according to the odometer Meeker had affixed to the wagon. In town, the Commercial Club grasp his plan with enthusiasm, provided the funds to inscribe a stone monument which was installed and dedicated on March 31. It was a grand party for Meeker reported over a thousand people showed up.

In Pendleton he purchased "a small Kodak." He removed heavy equipment from the wagon to lighten the load for traversing the Blue Mountains. These included his iron stove, his stereopticon* and miscellaneous other heavy plunder.

That evening he drove six miles out of town to an Indian School where he pulled in for the night. Having off-loaded his stove, he spent a miserable night due to the cold weather and "a scant supper." On the

*The stereopticon was also called a "magic lantern" and was used to project images from 3¼x4-inch glass slides on a large sheet hung on a wall. It was an early day slide projector. Whether Meeker's slide outfit was electric or lighted with pressurized oil, like a modern Coleman lantern, has not been established.

34

In 1906, Meeker's oxen and wagon had to be helped over the "Blues" by a team of sturdy horse due to a fresh, deep snow. When this picture was made, 1910, Meeker's only challenge seems to have been mud.

sunrise he went in to the school where he received a friendly reception and was allowed to use a room with a stove. ˊ¹

It appears up to 18-inches of snow had covered the Blue Mountains during the night and he had mixed feelings about proceeding into them under that condition. He had the usual "no, don't do it," "it will be impossible," etc, but others said it would be a "hard job." Meeker recorded:

I thought I best go [see for] myself, investigate on the spot and not run my neck into [trouble]. That evening [I went to] Meacham by rail and I was dumped off in the snow near midnight, no visible light in hotel nor track beaten to it and again the ardor of cold—cold, cold. Morning confirmed that 20 inches of snow had fallen. [I met] a sturdy mountaineer of long experience up there and one who had a team. On my [query] if he could help me across with his team said, "yes—it's possible to make it but I warn it will be a hard job." So the arrangement was made at once that the second morning after our meeting, his team would leave Meacham on the way to meet me.

Before Meeker left Meacham, he discussed setting a monument there for Meacham is an historic place with Lee's Encampment in

35

Meacham's monument was sponsored by the folks in Pendleton who wanted to help the few persons living in the mountain community. Meacham is reached today by I-84.

sight. Jason Lee, the first missionary to the Oregon Country, with four assistants, camped here in September 1834 as he supposed at the summit of the Blue Mountains. Since that time the little open area in the forest had been known as Lee's Encampment. (Now there is an Oregon State Park there named Emigrant Springs State Park.)

The man Meeker was talking with at Meachem, a Mr. Burns, agreed that an Oregon Trail marker should be placed there but exclaimed there was no money and declared, "but plenty of brawn. Send us a stone and I'll warrant you the foundation will be built and the monument put in place. "

Meeker took the next westbound train back to Pendleton to retrieve his team and wagon. In town he appealed for aid to provide an inscribed stone for Meacham to which he received a warm response. The stone was ordered.

The pull up the Blue Mountains was a chore. That night Meeker inscribed in his journal:

Camp No. 3 April 4 [1906]. We are now on the snow line of the Blue Mountains (8 p.m.) and am writing this by our first real out-of-door campfire under the spreading boughs of a friendly pine tree. We estimate have driven 12 miles, started from the [Indian] school at 7 a.m. the first three to four miles over a beautiful farming country, and then began climbing the foothills, up, up, up four miles and soon again up, reaching the first snow at 3 o'clock. The long up-hill pull fagged the Dave ox so we had to wait for him although I had given him an inch advantage on the yoke. True to promise, the team met us but not till we had reached the snow, axle deep and had the shovel in use to clear the way. By 3 P.M. [*sic.*] we were safely encamped at Meacham with the cheering news that the monument had arrived and could be dedicated the next day. So, the snowfall had proved a blessing in disguise as otherwise there would not have been a monument provided for Meacham.

By 11 the next morning the monument was in place with a ceremony, that included an orator from Pendleton. The little school at Meacham had turned out with its student body, a spectacle surely of an old man and a covered wagon and the dedication of a monument to the glories of the past.

When it was over, the two teams, the borrowed horses and the ox team, moved out for the summit which, of course, had not been reached with the worst tug ahead. Getting through the snow was very troublesome but at last they pitched camp on the east side of the mountain with LaGrande to be the next stop.

There were cheerful words awaiting on arrival in town. "Yes, we will have a monument." A stone was procured and Meeker wrote that a dedication ceremony was held to everyone's delight.

On April 11 he left LaGrande and brought with him in the wagon

The turnout at Ladd Canyon included many of the school children who took part in the dedication. This is one of few known pictures of Ezra Meeker not wearing his hat. (See page 38.)

ERECTED APRIL 19, 1906,
BY THE CITIZENS OF BAKER CITY
TO PERPETUATE
THE MEMORY OF THE

OLD OREGON TRAIL

AND TO HONOR THE INTREPID
PIONEERS WHO ESTABLISHED A
PROVISIONAL GOVERNMENT AND
WRESTED OREGON FROM
BRITISH RULE

Left page: Baker City. Meeker, holding fresh flowers, poses at the newly planted monument. Person at right not identified. Monument (lower) with Meeker's wagon in 1906. Picture on right made in May 1992. This page: Ezra Meeker with his outfit on Main Street, Baker City.

> At Baker City there was a wave of general enthusiasm and many lingered for a photograph of Old Timers, many with tears in their eyes due to this impromptu reunion and recollection of their own days on the Old Oregon Trail.

an inscribed stone to set up at an intersection near the mouth of Ladd's Canyon eight miles from LeGrande.

When he got to that point, nearby school children came in a body as well as several residents. The children sang, *Columbia the Gem of the Ocean* after which Meeker talked to them about the Old Oregon Trail. When the talking was finished, everyone sang *America—My County ''tis of Thee* then each child picked a stone from the roadway and cast it upon the pile surrounding the base of the monument.

After an overnight camp, on the morning of April 12, the Twist ox kicked Meeker in the right leg (some accounts say in the knee) and almost disabled him. Apparently he was laid up for a few days but pained much longer.

The people of Baker City were very willing to erect a monument on the high school grounds to perpetuate the memory of the trail even though the trail was six miles out of town on Flagstaff Hill and the

On the Centennial of the Oregon Trail (1943), the Kiwanis Club of Baker City (top) dedicated their Oregon Trail Monument. It is on Highway 86 five miles east of town near Flagstaff Hill. The spectacular Oregon Trail Interpretive Center atop Flagstaff Hill (lower left) opened in May 1992. (See page 76.) Meeker Monument (lower right) is just east of the Interpretative Center on north side of highway.

Virtue Flat to the east. (Some years later the monument was moved to a new city park where it can now be seen. This is across the street from the Oregon Trail Regional Museum.) For the Baker City turn-out, some 2,000 people came including some 800 school children. The children contributed a total of $60 in pennies and nickels for the monument. This was on April 19.

Sixteen miles and two days later at Straw Ranch, Meeker set an inscribed stone at a place called Old Mount Pleasant. But here, as at a few other places, everyone was not friendly toward Meeker and his ideas for preserving the trail. He met the owner of the place where Meeker wanted to place the marker—usually in a public highway— and he asked the man for a contribution. But the man refused and only gave Meeker scant courtesy. But nearby, some young people on seeing the wagon and hearing something of the discussion, dug into pockets and came up with the cost of the stone and $6 extra.

That night a tent, having been erected, was filled with people talking about the project until 9 P.M.

The next morning, while the stone was being implanted, five young men approached and volunteered to help with the work to complete the job.

Meeker pushed on as quickly as polite and possible after each stone's placement. The people at Durkee had heard what was going on and realizing their village was the next place where Meeker would arrive, greeted him with enthusiasm and declared they were ready to provide funds for a monument. A stone was ordered from the granite works in Baker City to be installed in the highway at Durkee. Having reached all the agreements with the townsfolk, Meeker moved out along the trail.

At Huntington, the 76 school children brought together the sum of over $4 in "dimes and half-dimes." Meeker was very encouraged with his results, realizing he was not yet anywhere near across the country. The huge turnout at Baker City impressed him very much. The attitude of most folks with whom he came in contact was gratifying. He wrote:

I am convinced this feature of the work is destined to give great results. It is not the financial aid I refer to but the effect it has upon children's minds to set them to thinking of this subject that has heretofore laid dormant, and to kindle a flame of patriotic sentiment that will endure in after life. Each child feels he has a part ownership in the shaft [they] helped pay for.

When he got to Vale, it was not a question of whether the people wanted a monument, but of what kind of stone it would be made. Local pride prevailed and the monument was erected from nearby rock. This was not as durable as granite, but everyone was happy. Seventy school children turned out and contributed to the fund and saw the shaft installed on the court house grounds. It was April 30.

At this point Meeker crossed the Snake River making an end of his work in the State of Oregon.

Ezra Meeker and his driver, Wm. Mardon (top), were well received in Boise. The Boise monument, (lower left) with Meeker, note wagon in background, in 1906. Marker (lower, right) as it appeared in 1987.

Chapter 10
His Idaho Experience

Now in Idaho, he went to the site of old Fort Boise. The fort, which was established as a stronghold of the Hudson's Bay Company in 1834 to thwart the efforts of American fur interests, also in 1834, at Fort Hall.

Some relics from Fort Boise were secured and arrangements made for a double-faced (inscribed) shaft to be installed at the site of the trail and of the Fort.

The first town encountered in Idaho was Parma, where contributions warranted shipping an inscribed stone from Boise City. Meeker left the arrangements to the City fathers who said it would be done.

Then he went on to Boise City. In Boise, the school officials were pleased to participate and collected nearly 1,200 contributions to the monument fund by students on the public schools, each child signing his or her name on a roll. This list showed the school and grade to which each child belonged. These rolls, with printed headings, were preserved and deposited with the Pioneer Society (now Idaho Historical Society). Each child was given a signed certificate showing the amount of the contribution.

> The citizens of Boise also paid for the stone planted on the site of the old fort and also for one installed on the Trail near the South Boise school buildings, all of which were native granite shafts, there being a large supply of granite available.

The Boise monument stands on the lawn of the State Capital and is inscribed as the children's' offering to the memory of the pioneers. Nearly 3,000 people attended the dedication service, published here to illustrate the zeal manifested here and in many other places as well.

PROGRAM PIONEER MONUMENT DEDICATION
CAPITOL GROUNDS - BOISE, IDAHO
Wednesday, May 9, 1906
Major J. A. Pinnet, Presiding

Song: *Idaho*

By the school children

A lovely mountain home is ours
Idaho, O, Idaho!
Of winters mild and springtime showers
Idaho, O, Idaho
Her breezes blow from western shore;
Where broad Pacific's billows roar;
Each year we love her more and more,
Idaho, O. Idaho

Her mountains grand are crowned with snow,
Idaho, O, Idaho!
And valleys fertile spread below,
Idaho, O, Idaho!
The towering pines on cliffs so steep,
O'er cataracts their vigils keep.
Or in the lakes mirrored deep,
Idaho, O, Idaho!

Invocation — Dean Hinks

Address — F. R. Coffin

Unveiling Monument
  Esther Gregory, Louise Morrison, Edna Perrault, Elizabeth Hays
Song *The Star Spangled Banner* — Male Quartet
  P. E. Tate, C. R. Davis, L. W. Thrailkill, M. R. McFerrin
Presentation of behalf of the school —Prof. J. E. Williamson
Address — Ezra Meeker
  The "Trail Maker" of Puyallup, Washington
Hymn: *America* — The Audience

My country 'tis of Thee,
Sweet land of liberty,—
  Of Thee I sing:
Land where my fathers died,
Land of the pilgrims' pride,
From every mountain side
  Let freedom ring!

My native country, thee,—
Land of the noble, free,—
  Thy name I love:
I love they rocks and rills,
Thy woods and templed hills;
My heart with rapture thrills
  Like that above.

Our fathers' God, to thee,
Author of liberty,—
  To thee we sing:
Long may our land be bright
With freedom's holy light;
Protect us by thy might,
  Great God, our King.

Meeker proceeded on down the trail and at Twin falls, 537 miles from The Dalles, money was contributed to place an inscribed stone in the track of the Old Trail a mile from the city therefore, a granite shaft was ordered.

At American Falls, now 649 miles out, an arrangement was made to erect a concrete shaft twelve feet high in the middle of the Old Trail the shaft to be surrounded by a park. (Years later, when the Snake River was dammed at American Falls, the marker and park were lost.)

The Ladies Study Club of Pocatello undertook the responsibility of erecting a marker on the high school grounds. Meeker wrote:

> [In Pocatello] I made 23 addresses to the school children on behalf of the work before leaving [town], and have the satisfaction of knowing the undertaking has been vigorously prosecuted and that a fine monument will soon be in place on the high school grounds.

The next place where an effort was made to erect a monument was 739 miles from The Dalles, at Soda Springs. A committee was formed to undertake the work, collect the money for a monument which was to be placed next to one of the bubbling soda springs. This was in a park on the Trail. A reclamation project has covered many of the old hissing and popping springs therefore little of the springs can be seen today. Just west of Soda Springs was the main turnoff from the Oregon Trail for those wanting to go to California's gold fields starting in 1849.

On June 7, he got up at 4:30 A.M. and was on the road in one hour. After proceeding a little way, his oxen were viciously attacked by a bull that was roaming through the hills. The bull attacked first from one side then from the other eventually getting himself between the two oxen which caused the team to nearly upset the wagon. It was exciting but dangerous. He wrote in his journal:

> I was finally thrown down in the melee but escaped unharmed. But it was a narrow escape from being run over by my team, [the bull] and the wagon.

Montpelier proved no exception to what was becoming almost a rule. Word was now passing along the trail that the old man with the covered wagon was on the way. When this news swept into a town, a committee would be appointed by the Commerical Club to see about erecting a suitable monument. By the time Meeker got into Montpelier, a collection of some $30 had already been paid into the fund by businessmen and citizens. While he was there, a meeting was called of the women's club which met in the Hunter Hotel, where Ezra Meeker had taken a room.* The ladies passed a resolution to thoroughly canvas the town for help with the project that would include getting the school children involved.

---

*It should be pointed out that Meeker carried a complete camping outfit in the wagon which included a tent, the heavy iron stove and foodstuffs for he often spent the night, and many

The Montpelier monument stands uncluttered on a pleasant residential street corner

When he went into Wyoming and stopped at Cokeville, he was 800¼ miles from the official start at The Dalles, Oregon. He had now crossed two states, Oregon and Idaho.

At Cokeville, on the Bear River, elevation 6,191 feet, he was getting into the higher elevations of the Oregon Trail. At Cokeville, he was well received by the business people who resolved to have a monument there. This would be on the Sublette Cut-Off where it joins the main trail coming from the south. After the local committee agreed to the plan, Ezra Meeker headed out of town and through western Wyoming's beautiful, green, mountains before reaching the Continental Divide at South Pass.

"noonings" on the trail away from civilization. But when he was in a town of any size overnight, he usually took a hotel room. It is not clear if Meeker paid for all of these room rents or, if he was a guest of the hotel keeper or of the Commercial Club/Chamber of Commerce or other organization, or if an individual picked up his bill. We are also aware he had a driver so accomodations had to be made for the driver as well. Meeker does not often mention the driver but William Mardon, a strong, young man, joined the expedition at The Dalles. In the fracus with the wild bull before arriving at Montpelier, Meeker's journal implies he, Meeker, is alone for no driver is mentioned. But Meeker, during his hop farming days, was a man of means and had many people working for him and he did not often mention them. His habit of no mention prevails on this trip. Some of the scenes of himself and team on the trail had to have a photographer. This may have been Mardon. But suppose his "Kodak" had a "delay action timer," as many cameras of that period did? This feature allowed him, if he was alone, to set the camera on a rock, or some such, rig the timer spring then he would run to get into position before the spring tripped the shutter and the picture was made.

Chapter 11
Walking Across The Rocky Mountains, Wyoming and Nebraska

From the town of Cokeville, Meeker proceeded eastward into a land where the elevations reach over 7,000 feet. This is an area of very little vegetation, where the wind blows nearly all the time and where there were few permanent residents in 1906 and only a few even today. One can stop, be perfectly still, and enjoy no sound other than one's own breathing. This is a land of grandeur. The air is clean and in the high altitude the weather may be brisk, even on a clear summer day.

Meeker's question to himself: "Why mark this trail?" often rang through his head. Here he was, a lone person in a solitude away from all civilization in an area where there were no roads—no travelers. Parts of it are not much different today. He answered his question by reminding himself of the driving force behind his venture. That force was to mark the Oregon Trail so it would become a monument to all who traveled over it and a memorial to the thousands who died along the way. He often had to remind himself of the mission when the going was tough realizing he might otherwise be at home where he could at least get a hot bath. But Ezra Meeker was an adventurer. Here was a man who felt the need to keep on the move. And in retracing the Old Oregon Trail, he moved along one foot after the other not much more than 2 miles in an hour.

Toward the end of June he arrived at Pacific Springs—not exactly a bustling metropolis for it registered only 25 people with maybe one hundred more scattered on far-flung ranches. The hamlet had a small general store in which there had been a post office since 1900. He recorded:

Pacific Springs, Wyoming. Camp No. 79, June 20, 1906. Odometer 958 miles (from The Dalles, Oregon). Arrived at 6:00 P.M. and camped near Halter's Store and the Post Office. Ice formed in camp during the night. Remained in camp all day [of the 21st and 22nd] and searched for a suitable stone for a monument to be placed at the summit. After almost despairing, I suddenly came to exactly what was wanted and although alone on the mountain side exclaimed, 'That is what I want; that's it.' So, after procuring help, we turned it over to find both sides were flat, with 26 inches face and

The large flat stone Meeker found on the side of the mountain was engraved then planted as a monument. Some years later it was remounted as shown in author's 1987 picture (right).

15 inches thick at one end and 14 inches wide and 12 inches at the other—one of nature's own handiwork as if made for this very purpose to stand at the top of the mountains for the centuries to come to perpetuate the memory of the generations that have passed.

Meeker hitched his team to Halter's wagon and, with four men from the small community, loaded the stone after they'd dragged it about 100 yards down the mountain to the wagon. Meeker estimates the weight of this stone, which was largely granite with some quartz, at about 1,000 pounds.

The next day, still in camp, Ezra set about inscribing the stone. He recalled:

The clerk of the store formed the letters on stiff paste board and then cut them out to make a paper stencil after which the shape of the letters was transferred to the stone by crayon marks. The letters were then cut with the cold chisel deep enough to make permanent inscription. The stone is so very hard that it required steady work all day to cut the twenty letters and figures, 'The Old Oregon Trail, 1843-57."*

On June 24, Meeker and his volunteers from Pacific Springs, planted the marker on the summit of South Pass at a location determined by civil engineer, John Lind, as

42°21' North Latitude 108°.53' West Longitude
Bearing N. 47, E. 240 feet from the ¼-corner between
Sections 4 and 5. Twnshp 27 North, Range 101 West of the 6 P.M.
Elevation determined by aneroid June 24, 1906: 7,450 feet**

On the 24th of June, Meeker and his new friends drove from his camp at Pacific Springs at 12:30 then stopped at the summit to dedicate the monument. While there, one of the fellows borrowed Meeker's camera and made a picture. Meeker recorded that the distance from Pacific Springs camp to the summit of South Pass was 12½ miles.

Meeker was seized with nostalgia when he reached the Sweetwater River:

I remember the sparkling, clear water, the great skirt of under-growth along the banks and the restful camps as we trudged along up the stream so many years ago. And now I see the same channel, the same hills, the same waters swiftly passing, but where are the campfires, where are the herds of gaunt cattle...the hallowing for lost children; the curse of irate ox drivers, the harsh sounds from some violin in camp, or the little groups off on the hillside to bury the dead? [It's] all gone. An oppressive silence prevailed as we drove down to the river and pitched camp within a few feet of the bank.

When he realized he was about mid-way on his trip over the old trail, Meeker decided to take a couple of days for rest. During the layover, only three persons passed that way. Then he recalled traveling for a week along here and met only five persons but only one wagon.

On June 30, he camped at a house at the famous split rock, a

*Meeker obviously guessed at the dates for the period of the Oregon Trail migrations extended well after 1857.

**Franzwa, writing in his *The Oregon Trail Revisited,* provides this data: "Four decades later, when the U.S. Geological Survey engineers were surveying the divide, they found that the precise location had been missed by less than 50 feet."

trail-side landmark. This was one of Meeker's favorite places along the Oregon Trail and he liked to stop and visit. In the house was a new post office, Sun, Wyoming, having been operating only three months. Its name, "Sun," is reported to have been the postmaster's name, "Thompson" broken by error into Tom Sun by a Post Office Department Clerk. It was the first mailing location for 85 miles from Pacific Springs. Sun was one-half mile to the upper end of the Devil's Gate.

Meeker recalled that in his memory, the most remarkable natural landmarks along the trail were Chimney, Jailhouse and Courthouse Rocks and Scotts Bluff in Nebraska and Independence Rock and Devil's Gate, both in Wyoming. The latter were just a few miles east of his camp at the split rock.

There is a certain likeness when looking at both Devil's Gate and the split rock. Both seem to have been cleaved by a huge ax striking the ridge of the mountains with the blow leaving v-shaped clefts. Of course at the split rock, the "cut" is to only slight depth when compared with Devil's Gate where the cleft—483 feet deep from the highest point—goes all the way to the Sweetwater River which runs through this "gate." The gorge is about 1,300 feet long with walls not quite perpendicular and in periods of high water in the spring of the year, there is often no space for anything to squeak through this rift in the mountain other than the river. People, even today, on approaching Devil's gate from the east, believe the road goes right through this cleft. But close to the rock, the highway veers away and goes around on the south side.

When Meeker was there in 1906, he:

> Clambered through on the left bank over boulders head high, under shelving rocks where sparrows' nests were in full possession, and ate some ripe wild gooseberries from bushes growing on the border of the river and plucked some beautiful wild roses on the 2nd day of July, A.D. 1906. I longed to see this place, for here, somewhere under the sands lies all that was mortal of a brother, Charles Meeker, who drowned in the Sweetwater in 1854 while attempting to cross the plains.

The following day Meeker pushed on eastward to Independence Rock. The rock, which loosely resembles a huge whale quietly taking a nap, is six miles from Devil's Gate. The rock is 193 feet elevation above the plain and is 1,950 feet long by 850 feet wide.

Meeker took quite a bit of time looking at the thousands of names scratched on the great rock, which has been called the pioneer guest register.

Author Bert Webber on top of Independence Rock during convention field trip of Oregon-California Trails Association in 1987.

Independence Rock

To gain the top, one must pass through a gate near the parking lot at the roadside interpretive exhibit and proceed to the back, the side away from the highway. The climb to the top is not difficult for the sure-footed remembering wind gusts are frequent and can be dangerous. Leather soles on shoes can be slippery on rocks. Anyone trampling in the outback must be alert for pesky Wyoming rattlesnakes which are numerous in the area.

Sweetwater River viewed in an easterly direction from on top of Independence Rock.

Meeker selected a place on the rock where he, with his dulled cold chisel and a hammer, cut letters for his inscription "Old Oregon Trail 1843-1857." Then with some "sign-writers paint in oil" he painted the letters in the hope they would last. He commented that his poor chisel was not capable of deeper engraving.

His travel was not without risks and danger remembering Ezra Meeker was no young, sprightly adventurer but in his 76th year. Sprightly for his age, certainly, but nevertheless old and worn.

He recalled his stop at Fish Creek eleven miles east of Independence Rock saying he observed the creek was crammed with fish. As fresh fish would be a welcome change in diet, but without any net to catch any, he took a blanket and attempted to seine them. While working at this project he stepped into a hole and took water over the top of his boots. He journaled: "I worked all the noon hour instead of resting as like an elderly person should...." He ended with wet feet, wet socks, wet blanket and apparently never did catch any fish, all of these negatives not contributing very positively to his trip of the remainder of the day.

By the close of the day on the 5th of July, he made "Camp No. 89, North Platte River, 15 miles above the town of Casper. Odometer 1,104 miles from The Dalles."

52

Ezra Meeker at Independence Rock in 1906

Pesky Wyoming Rattlesnakes
During that day he, and his driver, William, observed heavy black clouds, distant lightning, and rumbling thunder. Thunder storms on the plains in summer are common. And the wind came up fiercely. But it did not rain on them. The excitement of the day was of a different nature:

This afternoon as we were driving, with both [of us] in the wagon, William heard the rattles of a snake and jumped out of the wagon and thoughtlessly called the dog. I stopped the wagon and called the dog [Jim] away from the reptile until it was killed. When stretched out it measured four feet, eight inches and had eight rattles.

On the next day, on nearing Casper, he heard the whistle of a locomotive for the first time in 300 miles. After lunch, he walked ahead into town to get his mail and to arrange for feed for his team. At the post office there were twenty letters including several from home.

Back in 1852 it was during lunch break when repairs were made, hubs greased and women did as much advance cooking as possible. Meeker's wagon did not need fixing and as he did little cooking, he spent noon times writing his book.

He also called on the Commercial Club and after talking with the office man, a special meeting was called for that night. Meeker wrote:

I laid the matter of building a monument before them with the usual result. They resolved to build one and opened the subscription at once, and appointed a committee to carry the work forward. I am assured by several prominent citizens that a $500 monument will be erected as the city council will join with the club to provide a fountain as well, and place it on the most public street-crossing of the city.

At Glen Rock, where he arrived after darkness fell after a twenty-five mile trek—the longest single day drive of this trip—he met with the ladies club which decided "they would have as nice a monument as Casper" even if it would not cost as much. One reason for the lower cost was the nearness, six miles from town, of a stone quarry. One of the ladies declared with great emotion and enthusiasm, "we will inscribe it ourselves if no stone-cutter can be found."

As he left "the nice little burg and said goodby to the energetic ladies in it" he said half-aloud to himself, "Where there's a will there's a way." Then with his own emotions flowing he wrote:

54

God bless the women anyhow. I don't see how the world could get along without them and anyway, I don't see what life would have been to me without that faithful companion that came over this same ground with me fifty-four years ago and still lives to rejoice for the many, many blessings vouchsafed to us and our descendants.

By the time he reached Douglas, Wyoming, he was 1,177½ miles out of The Dalles, Oregon.

In Douglas he determined that his plan was falling on many a deaf ear for everyone was "too busy" to spend any time on a monument project. But some were willing to give a little money. Meeker engaged in a short, probably door-to-door, canvas and collected $52. Finally, he was able to get a few people together to form a committee and assume responsibility in an organized manner for a monument project. It took some persuasion at Douglas. In his journal he wrote he needed to be sure the project "was well in hand before we drove out of town."

At Douglas he at last caught up with the roving thunderstorm, or one might say the storm caught up with him. He was reminded of the heavy downpours of 1852 where, in the case of his being in Douglas:

The water came down in veritable sheets and in an incredibly short time turned all the slopes into roaring torrents and level places into lakes. The water ran six inches deep in the streets.

On down the road in Camp No. 95, he was camped under shade trees on the North Platte River near the bridge at a company farm where a Dr. J. M. Wilson was superintendent. He was invited to have his fill of vegetables. This was the first fresh-from-the-farm feast in hundreds of miles. He enjoyed the gift and was welcome to carry extra with him to last several days.

His supper menu:

> Calf's liver, fried crisp with bacon
> Young onions
> Boiled young carrots
> Beets covered with vinegar
> Lettuce with vinegar and sugar
> Crisp radishes
> Cornmeal mush, cooked 40 minutes
> (with reserve for a breakfast fry)
> Coffee with cream and a lump of butter

On July 16 he came to Fort Laramie and noted his odometer was at 1,247. Recalling his trek in 1852, he mentioned that Fort Laramie

19. Chimney Rock, near Bayard,
    North Platte, Neb.

CHIMNEY ROCK

Rising 470 feet above the North Platte River Valley, Chimney Rock stands to the south as the most celebrated of all natural formations along the overland routes to California, Oregon, and Utah. Chimney Rock served as an early landmark for fur traders, trappers, and mountain men as they made their way from the Rockies to the Missouri River. To later emigrants, the solitary spire marked the end of plains travel and the beginning of the rugged mountain portion of their journey.

The tip of the formation is 325 feet above the base. Chimney Rock is composed of Brule Clay with interlayers of volcanic ash and Arickaree sandstone. Thousands of travelers carved their names in the soft base only to have these records disappear through the forces of nature. This eroded landmark is smaller than that which greeted early visitors to the area, but its presence for the generations of the near future is secure.

In 1941 the eighty acres containing the site were transferred to the Nebraska State Historical Society by the Roszel F. Durnal family. In 1956 Norman and Donna Brown deeded additional land to the Society. In that same year Chimney Rock was designated a National Historic Site by the federal government.

Nebraska State Historical Society

Left page: Chimney Rock as it was in 1906 (top) with Meeker's outfit in foreground and (center) as it was in 1987 with rich Nebraska corn field in foreground. Courthouse Rock and Jail house Rock (lower) are nearby.
This page: Jail house Rock with typical summer thundercloud in back. The pioneers held these landmarks in great wonder and nearly all who kept a diary mentioned them.

was the mid-point goal to be reached by thousands of pioneers. It was also the last place where mail could be claimed or sent.

Meeker experienced occasional inconvenience with his persnickety team and their menu. While many cattle will eat whatever is being fed, or have access to in the field, his team ate the grass before them in the evening but would not feed on the same plot in the morning. Yet the cattle would not travel without eating grass and poked along stopping to munch grass from the middle of the road. After going a scant two miles and finding good grass, he turned them out to eat. Finally, as if they could talk, the animals indicated they were filled.

But that's not the end of the tale. Now full, they were lazy and would hardly move. Accordingly, Meeker became exasperated. Finally the team could be made to move but he had to quit at 4 o'clock in the afternoon. The day had been a very hot one with the summer sun showing no mercy. It had not been a good day on the road.

It was not many miles before he was in front of one of the great landmarks of the plains, Scotts Bluff near the town of Scottsbluff, Nebraska. The bluff rises 800 feet above the flat prairie and is today a National Monument with an intense tourist season.

> **A paved road allows tourists to drive to the top of Scottsbluff where there is an interpretive center and impressive view of the land for hundreds of miles. Access is from the town of Gering across the North Platte River from Scottsbluff.**

Ezra Meeker's tour of 1906 took him through Bayard,* Nebraska on the North Platte River where ruts of the Old Oregon Trail can be clearly seen today. From here he went to Chimney Rock which he called "a curious freak of nature." It rises 470 feet above the river.

The base of Chimney Rock reminds one of an umbrella resting on the ground with handle pointing up—200 feet up to the base with the spire resting on it. The spire (chimney) points to the heavens as a church spire, tall and slim. Meeker declared, "The wonder of it—how it comes the hand of time has not leveled it long ago.

There is a yarn local folks like to tell about the spire having been

---

*Just out of Bayard, on Highway 26, Gordon and Patti Howard operate "The Oregon Trail Wagon Train." This is a unique business where visitors can enjoy rides in covered wagons in ruts of the old Oregon Trail. One route goes over to Chimney Rock. The rides last from 2 hours and trail campouts up to 6 days. Every evening patrons enjoy "chuckwagon cookout" in the outdoor dining area followed by a songfest around a campfire. When the OCTA convention was in Scottsbluff, about 400 of these trail buffs called Gordon and arranged to come over for buffalo stew dinner.

much taller but a young artillery officer, wanting to show off the marksmanship of his battery, used Chimney Rock for target practice and shot off the top. Meeker mentions this tale in his 1906 book, and the authors heard it related during the 1987 convention of the Oregon-California Trails Association at Scottsbluff. Folklore?

Meeker was greeted at the town of North Platte by the ladies of the Women's Christian Temperance Union—most of the business men refusing to give of their time. The women were enthused with his plans and success in other towns. Not wanting to be outdone, they appointed a committee to erect a monument. When Mr. W. C. Ritner heard what was going on, he stepped forward and offered to donate a monument. It would be mounted on a concrete base with marble cap, the stone and concrete column to be 5½ feet tall. The offer was graciously accepted.

Without any suspicion that he was in ill health, Meeker's ox, Twist, took suddenly sick and within two hours was dead. (Meeker later believed the ox might have eaten some toxic trail-side plant)

Meeker was faced with the need for a decision on these questions: What should he do? Abandon the trip due to loss of half his pulling power? Were there any oxen for sale in the vicinity of his location?

He sought a farmer whom he could hire with a team of horses to at least get to the next town. This was Gothenburg, thirteen miles away. His remaining ox was trailed on a line behind the wagon. At Gothenburg he immediately set about with his monument erection project. It was August 10. The people in that town decided to erect a marker and formed a committee for taking action. Immediately, $15 was raised toward the work.

He released the team and hired another for the haul into Lexington. The distance was about 25 miles. On arrival there he went about locating the owner of a herd of about 200 cows he learned about. This was because of his recollection from his 1852 trip when he'd seen many wagons being pulled by cows. The local folks couldn't believe it when he said he would pull his wagon with *cows*.

He bought two very large cows. Alas, one of the cows refused to move even one inch when yoked. After considerable experimentation, he went back to the farmer and begged for a trade. The swap was made but not to Meeker's financial satisfaction. Nevertheless, he had to be on his way for in Lexington he was "rebuffed by a number of businessmen" who complained they had no time to be involved with a monument project.

At Kearney, he was accorded the very best place in town for his campsite where people came in great numbers to express their approval for the monument project. Meeker had every reason to believed his crusade in Kearney would yield a large, attractive permanent monument. But when he talked to business men, all were "too busy." Even the President of the Commercial Club refused to call a meeting stating he had no time and felt all the business men were also otherwise occupied.

Meeker mused:

As I left this man's office, who, I doubted not had spoken the truth, I wondered to myself if these busy men would ever have time to *die?* I did not however feel willing to give up the work. I had traveled 1,700 miles with only about 200 more miles to go. I will try Grand Island.

Ezra Meeker was down in the heart about his rebuff when he could not even find three people in Lexington for a committee then had been equally rebuffed in Kearney. But he recalled his experience of the last several months where he had traveled a great distance and met many people. He smiled as he took stock:

19 monuments in place or promised
12 or more boulders including the great
    Independence Rock had been inscribed
100 temporary wooden poles alongside roads
    awaiting permanent markers
Over 3,000 school children had contributed
    pennies and nickels toward monuments
Over 20,000 people had turned out to
    hear him speak and to attend dedications

Most of the time Meeker was a positive thinker about his situations. As he plodded along now in Central Nebraska on an unmercifully hot summer day, be awakened from his present troubles with his own inspiration, "Do the best you can and do not be cast down." He wrote following that thought: "My spirits rose almost to the point of exultation."

When he arrived at Grand Island, on the 30th of August, he set up his camp under the trees and commenced his meetings with a single person here, a few more there. Then some more over here, and then there. This was Meeker's way of "suggestive selling." In a few days he completed arrangements for a monument to be installed at Grand Island.

Meeker concludes his 1906 journal in these words:

At Grand Island I shipped to Fremont, Nebraska to head the procession celebrating the semi-centennial of founding that city, working the ox and cow together; thence to Lincoln, where the first edition of [my] book was printed. All the while I was searching for an ox without avail. Finally, after looking over a thousand head of cattle in the stock yards at Omaha, a four-year-old steer was found and broken in on the way to Indianapolis, where I arrived January 7, 1907, eleven months and seven days from date of departure from my home in Puyallup, 2,600 miles distant.

THE OREGON TRAIL
ILLUSTRATED BY 25 POST CARDS
With Story on Reverse Side of Each.
25 Postcards for 25 Cents.

Reproduction of envelope (reduced image for this book) in which Meeker packaged a set of 25 picture post cards which he sold for 25¢. The pictures were made during the 1906 trip and the cards printed in Lincoln, Nebraska before he continued on to the Atlantic Coast. As the trip progressed, Meeker was plagued with the same questions time and again so he printed this flyer which he and Mardon gave to passersby.

Before Asking Questions, Read!

These Oxen made trip to Washington, D. C. They are nine years old; Durhams. The droop-horn ox, Dave, weighs 1900 pounds; Dandy, the nigh ox, weighs 1700 pounds. Will travel 15 miles a day. Both were five-year-old range steers when broken in on this wagon for this trip. Aggregate gain in weight while on this trip, 920 pounds.

——— POST CARD VIEWS ———

SERIES A.—16 colored views of the Old Oregon Trail Monument Expedition..............25c
SERIES B.—8 plain views in this envelope...10c
SERIES C.—25 plain views...25c
    BOOKS:—The Tragedy of Leschi, $1.50 net; Ventures and Adventures, $1.00 net.

Address Ezra Meeker, Seattle, Wash.

Meeker attracted attention almost everywhere he went.
This scene is in Hebron, Nebraska

Addendum

While conducting his business in Lincoln, Ezra Meeker contracted with a printer to make his book, *Ox Team, or The Old Oregon
Trail 1852-1906*. This was the book on which he was writing while
stopped along the Trail. He also placed an order with the William-
Haffner Company, printers, Denver, to make "some [post] cards for
you by the cheap process."

After finishing the route over the trail at the Missouri River, he
visited several major cities trying to get support for his project.
Among these were Terre Haute, Indiana, Cleveland, Ohio and New
York City. The further east he went, the less interest was found a-
mong the people even though his outfit attracted much attention.

In New York City he ran up against an ordinance that prohibited
the driving of cattle on city streets. But, after considerable persuasion,
authorities made an exception thus we see Ezra Meeker surrounded by
thousands of people in his post card view of his outfit in Broad Street.

There must have been tens of thousands of snapshots made of
Meeker and of his wagon and oxen by early-day snapshot shooters for
amateur cameras were becoming popular. But of all the snapshots
made of Meeker on the streets, only a few got back as gifts as he was
always on the move. One is included in this section. Who took the

Meeker always tried to be in the forefront of his activities and is shown (top) in an unidentified automobile in an unnamed town. Lower picture was made in Omaha, Nebraska.

picture and in what city has not been learned.

Meeker's burning desire was to visit with the President of the United States. On learning that President Theodore Roosevelt was in Oyster Bay on Long Island, Meeker went there but apparently could not get in to see him. Much later, on November 29, he did meet the President and was assured that Mr. Roosevelt would support anything the Congress passed on his behalf. (House Bill No. 11,722, 1908, the "Humphrey Bill," sought $50,000 for "Marking the 'Old Oregon' Trail." It did not pass.)

Here is the very proud Ezra Meeker with his borrowed
Pathfinder Touring Car. His driver, with Meeker as pas-
senger, drove this vehicle from Washington D.C. to
Olympia, Washington between May 5, and September 12,
1916. This was the new 1916 model with 6.4-litre, 12
cylinder Weidley engine and 120-inch wheelbase. Location
where photographed not established.
— Data from *Complete Encyclopedia of Motorcars 1885-1968*. (Dutton 1968)

Ezra Meeker's visits to other major cities did not bring in the
support needed. Sale of his books and post cards, particularly in the
south, did not meet his expenses. His visits in Texas insofar as
gaining interest in his project he called a disaster.

He made another covered wagon and oxen trip in 1910-1911
during which he took more pictures to add to his post card collection.

In 1915 he let it be known he wanted to aggressively promote his
desire for the national highway. In this regard, Meeker visited with
President Woodrow Wilson who agreed with his proposal.

Also in this year, Meeker completed a deal with the Pathfinder
Company of Indianapolis, for the free use of one of their new touring
cars, and to receive a small cash weekly stipend ($15.00) for his
personal "expenses." The company set aside a car for the proposed
trip on which they custom-built a covered wagon top.

After the trip was under way, Meeker was admonished for not
staying on a "schedule" to visit Pathfinder dealers who were waiting
for him to show off the car at their dealerships. Meeker was apparently trying to kill two birds with one stone—use the car for his
own purposes in promoting the Oregon Trail as a national highway as
well as advertise the automobile for its manufacturer. It is obvious
that Pathfinder read more into the deal than Meeker did, the firm

20. *President Roosevelt viewing the Team, 1907.*

Ezra Meeker in Washington, D.C. (top) with his outfit at the White House, (lower) meeting with President Theodore Roosevelt near the end of Meeker's trip in 1907.

expecting lots of free publicity which they didn't think they were getting. But for historians, the trip was noteworthy due to the colorful correspondence it generated between him and the company's advertising department.

Meeker had the car for a considerable time, but inclusive dates are elusive. The Company had to pay the roadside expenses that included parts as well as gasoline (called "distillate" at this period)

4. *On the Street, Terre Haute, Ind. 1910.*

24. *Broad Street, near Wall, New York City. 1907.*

"On the Street, Terre Haute, Indiana" (top) The 1910 trip.
Pressed by a curious crowd (lower) in Broad Street near
Wall Street, New York's Financial District, in 1907

and oil ("l qt. oil 10¢"), which were considerable. As the Pathfinder
Company did not have a wide distribution, and only limited parts
availability, we find Meeker frequently carping for parts. After one
such complaint, the company retorts by Western Union Telegram
crisply declaring:

GASKETS FORWARDED GENERAL DELIVERY ON TWENTY THIRD PATHFINDER CO.

67

23. Ezra Meeker at Aviation Meet,
    Los Angeles, 1910.

Meeker's visit (top) to the Los Angeles Aviation Meet in 1910 was a sensation to the crowd comparing the covered wagon to the airplane. Of the countless snapshots (lower) made of Meeker by bystanders few have been found. This one was in Giffin, Ohio in front of Opera House in spring of 1911 "on the Saturday before Palm Sunday." That would have been on April 8. The snapshooter is not named.

Pathfinder's representative blasted Meeker several times in letters complaining that Meeker's driver was not "careful," especially when the car got stuck in the mud. The muddy roads surely validated the need for a suitable highway.

In 1924 Ezra Meeker got his chance to over fly the Oregon Trail when an Army pilot, Lt. Oakley G. Kelley received orders to carry

"The alamo" San Antonio. Tex. 1911.
mardon. *Sim.* *Ezra Meeker*

From his usual middle-of-the-country route, Meeker turned
south to visit the famous Alamo in Texas in 1911. This is
an original signed photograph made in a Department Store
darkroom in San Antonio. In left foreground is Wm. Mordon,
driver. Ezra Meeker is seated on his wagon just above his
signature. Meeker declared his trip to Texas found an in-
different crowd from which he did not meet expenses.

the old pioneer in his De Haviland airplane with its "great Liberty
Motor." This was big news because Kelly had been the first to fly
nonstop from coast to coast the year before. Meeker, now age 94, had
petitioned the War Department to go when he learned Lt. Kelly was
to fly from the West coast to Dayton, Ohio. The one special pre-
caution Meeker took, on climbing into the cockpit, was to put his
false teeth in his pocket just in case they might fall out of his mouth.

Meeker quipped on arrival in Boise a few hours later that he had
just traversed one-third of the trail between breakfast and lunch and
was making better time in the air than with the ox team.

By the time the plane landed in Omaha, the cross-country flight
had been in the air 13½ hours. On arrival in Dayton, Meeker "got his
enjoys" by being guest of honor with the pilot, riding in a special
open top car before the mile long grandstand of 40,000 people who
had gathered for the air races. On the reviewing stand, Ezra Meeker
was seated next to Orville Wright, the first person to pilot a plane. He
told Orville, "You'd be surprised at the difference between riding in a
Prairie Schooner and in an airplane."

Although Kelley's original orders were just to fly Meeker to

69

LANDING AT SPOKANE AFTER A FLIGHT OF 90 MILES FROM LEWISTON, IDAHO.

Meeker loved to fly. (Top) He and Lt. Oakley Kelley Landed at Spokane after a flight of 90 miles from Lewiston, Idaho. (Right) Kelley and Meeker.

Dayton, the great favorable publicity each received convinced the War Department to order Lt. Kelley to take Meeker all the way to his destination, Washington, D.C. The hop from Dayton to the nation's capitol took four hours. The total air time for the trip coast-to-coast was 24 hours during which they covered 2,700 miles.

On October 7, 1924, Meeker met with President Calvin Coolidge at the White House and unfolded his plan to make the Oregon Trail a national highway.

Meeker returned to Seattle by train.

In 1928, Henry Ford, President of the Ford Motor Company, which had just introduced its all new and ultimately internationally famous Model A Ford, directed that a sedan be converted to carry a prairie schooner top for Ezra Meeker's next trip. Mr. Ford wanted to help Meeker's pleas for the highway by using a Ford car for the trip. The idea was somewhat a repeat of the 1916 trip in the Pathfinder only now, 12 years later, there had been tremendous advances in automotive engineering and there was at least a fairly good road. The Model A was the latest, hottest car on the road. Regrettably, Meeker became ill and was hospitalized in Michigan at Henry Ford's expense. When Ezra Meeker was able to travel again, Mr. Ford bought train accommodations for the almost 98-year-old man and sent him home.

On arrival in Seattle, Meeker took a room at the Frye Hotel where he died four days later.

Ezra Meeker stands at side of the new 1928 Model A Ford preparing for his next cross-country trip just before he became ill. The highways across America were quite good by 1928 and the trip probably would have been without difficulty. As a youngster, author Bert Webber crossed the country in 1930 in a 1927 Chevrolet following highways 40, 87, 30 (Wyoming), 40 (now I-80) from St. Louis to San Francisco. The unhuried trip took about ten days.

Summary

As we have seen, Ezra Meeker opened his program for preserving the Old Oregon Trail with his west-to-east covered wagon trek in the spring of 1906. Then he followed with another west-to-east trip with his wagon and team in 1910. The purpose of this book is to show his great initial effort (1906) and to record, but not in detail, the other trips.

In 1916, on a deal made with Pathfinder Motor Car Company, he made the trip in a specially outfitted automobile. It was a modern, good idea that for the most part was only partially successful. This effort saw one of the first efforts for an auto that was trying to make a transcontinental trip under powerfully poor road conditions, lack of spare parts, misunderstandings between Meeker and the manufacturer with excuses from both sides that did not yield a satisfactory experience for either party. Not a lot has been written about this "Pathfinder Adventure" and we are unable, regrettably, to add very much more.

In 1922, Ezra Meeker visited Baker City and while there formed his famous Oregon Trail Memorial Association, the headquarters of which would be in New York City.

During the early 1920's Meeker became enthusiased with the idea of flying in an airplane and he made several local flight. He was one of the first passengers to fly transcontinental (Vancouver, Washington to Washington, D.C.) this event in 1924. The airplane was an open cockpit U.S. Army plane identified only by Meeker as a DeHaviland and it had a "great Liberty motor." *Jane's Encyclopedia of Aviation* (1989) is unclear but allows the plane was British made by the De-Haviland subsidiary "Airco" with this model D.H.9A(UK) "using the American built 298kW (400 hp) Liberty 12 [cyl] engine...."

Meeker traversed the Oregon Trail by these methods in these years:

Covered wagon	1852
Covered wagon	1906
Covered wagon	1910
Pathfinder automobile	1916
Railroad	Various
Army airplane	1924
Model A Ford	Trip planned for 1928 but due to Meeker's death was canceled.

The Ezra Meeker Historical Post Cards for Schools, Libraries, the Home and Collectors.

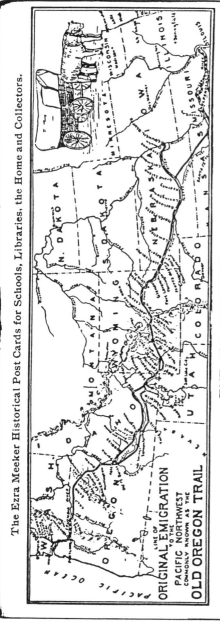

LINE OF
ORIGINAL EMIGRATION
TO THE
PACIFIC NORTHWEST
COMMONLY KNOWN AS THE
OLD OREGON TRAIL

THE OLD OREGON TRAIL.

The famous Trail, shown on the map, the natural gateway to the Pacific, may be said to date back to the discovery of the South pass of the Rocky Mountains in 1822 by Etienne Provost, although sections of it had been traversed by hardy adventurers in the early part of the seventeenth century.

After the buffaloes came the Indians, followed in turn by trappers and traders, and these by the intrepid missionaries who pointed the way for that mightiest migration of the world's history, the home builders of the Pacific Northwest, to the Oregon country. History does not record so great a movement for so great a distance as this, over a 2,000 mile stretch of an unknown country from the Missouri River to the Pacific coast. The Mormons in 1846 and the gold seekers of California in '49 followed the Oregon Trail for more than a thousand miles to the big bend of the Bear River and contended for possession of the single trail then existing, with the still passing throng to Oregon, until in later years parallel tracks were worn deep for long distances as the multitudes jostled each other in their weary westward journey.

The Oregon Trail is without its parallel of picturesque scenery, its tragedies and legends of heroism, that some day will lend a theme for an imperishable epic to go down into history for all ages, as has already been the physical marks along the way to point the spots where the multitudes passed and suffered and died.

74

The Ezra Meeker papers and history of his Oregon Trail preservation projects can be found in two major locations within a few miles. These are the Ezra Meeker Historical Society in the Meeker Mansion in Puyallup (see page 93) and in the archives of the Washington State Historical Society in Tacoma. These institutions are about six miles apart. Many of the Meeker family artifacts are in the mansion. Most of the Meeker papers, as well as his wagon and preserved pulling team are in the offices in Tacoma. The photograph on this page is of a study group of the Northwest Chapter of the Oregon-California Trails Association while visiting the Tacoma facility following a guided tour in the Meeker Mansion.

Oregon Trail Interpetive Center
Baker City, Oregon

The new Interpretive Center on Flagstaff Hill 6-miles east of Baker City, Oregon on Highway 86 is an authentic trail experience for visitors. The great hall contains life-size exhibits that are awe-inspiring. Two of the displays are shown here. The End-of-the-Trail Interpretive Center is in Oregon City.

James R. "Jim" Evans,
educator and historian.
He and Ezra Meeker were
friends and he recalls
Meeker's visit to Baker City
in 1922.

Hitting the Trail in 1992

When the planning was taking place for the dedication and grand opening celebration for the Interpretive Center on Flagstaff Hill, Jim Evans, a Baker County historian and educator, brought up a keen idea. As there are easily accessible and highly recognizable original Oregon Trail ruts leading up to Flagstaff Hill, his presentation was a plan for a "trail walk." The walk would start some miles out, allow participants to experience an overnight camp and cookout in the sage brush, then complete the trip and arrive at Flagstaff Hill in time for the ceremonies.

This plan had a lot going for it. There could be as many as four generations of people participating. The "walk" would be for people whose hobby was pioneering and who owned covered wagons and suitable pulling animals and might like to use them for such an event. It would be open to horsemen. It would be open to the every day sort of person who just wanted to walk the trail to have the experience.

Everywhere the plan was discussed it was met with enthusiasm. There was no prescribed costume. Those who wanted to wear current street clothing could do so (few did). The idea was wear clothing to identify with the pioneer period. This meant no jeans as well as other present contemporary attire.

When it came time for the "sign-up" and specific instructions for the trek, the turnout numbered about 400 persons. This was a lot of people who wanted to take a break from the whirling daily events in to which they are usually locked. There were bankers, farmers, law-

Ruts of the trail in vicinity of Oregon Trail Interpretive Center near Baker City, Oregon. The 1992 Oregon Trail Experience "walk"(as most participants did not have covered wagons to ride in) started 16-miles east of the Center then walked the trail. The first day was an 8-mile walk to an overnight camp site in the sage brush. On the the second day the participants continued to the Interpretive Center.

yers, gas station attendants, doctors, teachers, salespeople, truck drivers, home makers, musicians, the retired. The ages ranged from under one year to 84. There were folks with promises to bring their wagons, horses, mules, oxen. There would be "pioneer women," "pioneer men," "pioneer children." Some of the costumes were heirlooms that had been carefully stored in family trunks for decades. Most of the coon skin caps were hand made from the remnants of road kills.

Some of the participants were fanciers of black-powder mountain lore who planned to be in full costume and would bring their muskets.

These were not just local people, but folks who heard about the walk and came from across the state, from Washington and Idaho, and a few other places, who wanted to participate as much as possible in a "real" Oregon Trail experience. Many were descendants of pioneer families.

On the day set for the "rendezvous," all the participants met at a

At the 4-mile mark, the caravan of wagons, horsemen and walkers stopped to await arrival of the "lunch wagon"—the truck with catered food seen approaching in the cloud of dust.

point sixteen miles east of Flagstaff Hill. They arrived with friends to drive their automobiles, horse trailers, travel trailers and the like to a special parking lot near the end of the route. When all was in readiness, the caravan of 29 animal-pulled covered wagons, the horse people and the walkers moved out into the ruts of the Old Oregon Trail. They were led by a pair of U.S. Army Cavalry troopers, and their wagon, wearing uniforms of the time. It was a warm, comfortable, sunny day. The group spaced itself along the trail and plodded toward the west. The speed was the same as 150 years ago—about two miles in an hour.

Come time for "nooning," the very large group clustered and waited for the chuck wagon to appear. But no horse-drawn cooking cart was to be seen. But from off in the distance a present-day truck, loaded with catered goodies, arrived in a cloud of dust.

(Of course "nooning" in pioneer days was the time for the men to repair broken wagons, grease the hubs and other chores. The women's responsibility was to cook "dinner" and enough for supper if circumstances were favorable. On many a day the trek would continue until after nightfall and any supper would have to have been previously prepared and eaten cold. If the "nooning" was long enough and if there was water available, it would beproper to do the laundry.

People, horses and mules all stop for lunch in the sage
brush.

Walking the trail—1992.

In due time, and again in the plodding method of the original pioneers, the caravan moved out. Those toward the front ate less dust. As
the spring afternoon wore along the day was getting warmer. There
were many tired feet. Some kept on going, blisters and all. A few
reached into their packs and brought out a change of socks or shoes.
One woman, who administered her own first aid for aching feet,
stopped by trailside, took off her shoes and poured a canteen of cool
water on her feet. She let them air-dry; then with fresh socks, put her
shoes on, and continued on her way.

The rule of this trip was leave nothing behind but your footsteps.
There would be no litter along the trail in 1992.

This was a Bureau of Land Management program. In its wisdom,
the BLM had brought in dozens of Rangers from other Districts
throughout Oregon. These "guards" were posted to keep non-partici-
pants from distracting the activities of the wagon train.

Unlike the pioneers of the early days, cameras of all kinds were
common on the 1992 trek. Although photography made its first ap-
pearance in 1839, there were almost no pictures made along the trail
during the great migrations to the Oregon Country. For the present
adventure, several professional cameramen were among the hikers and
their challenge, from time-to-time, was to be certain amateur cameras
and video equipment were kept out of their pictures.

As evening came over the caravan, the wagon train pulled in to
the chosen location for the overnight stop. The wagons circled. The
animals were unyoked or unhooked from their lines. Farm supply

The musical concert at the lunch stop was by jew's harp.

Many youngsters were in this unique trail experience.

A major planner of the trail walk was James R. "Jim" Evans, Baker City, who was a friend of Ezra Meeker. He was Baker County Superintendent of Schools for 27 years. Jim, at 84, shown with daughter Mary Lynne Myer, walked all 16 miles.

firms had provided huge watering troughs which were full and in place for the animals.

Hours earlier, a crew of "cooks" had dug a fire trench where coals were by now glowing and fry pans were ready for the batter which would yield tasty and remarkably tender fried bread. Huge vats were bubbling with buffalo stew—meat, carrots, potatoes and a little onion floated in a somewhat watery, non-salty "soup" that was "just right" peppery flavored. The fragrance of this trail supper was carried on the evening breeze and settled in the noses of hungry "pioneers" who formed long lines in anticipation. And there were brown beans. And there was jam. And there was cool, cool fresh drinking water trucked in from Baker City, as contrasted with the tainted water the pioneers were often forced to drink of an earlier year.

Washing one's hands before eating was practically unheard
of during the great migration period and this oversight
condributed to death by cholera. On the 1992 trail walk,
portable wash basins, portable toilets, portable showers
were brought in for the overnight stop.

The participants enjoyed buffalo stew and brown beans with
griddle-fried bread for trail supper at end of first day's walk.

Jim, age 84, and Rachael, nine months, were the
oldest and youngest on the 1992 trail walk.

Jim Evans and the "well-dressed" pioneer.

After the first day's walk, the wagons circled and the modern-day walkers set up their tents. Row of objects in center are portable toilets, a feature that did not exist along the trail during the migration 150 years ago.

And there was coffee. Gallons of coffee from a huge urn that made the day for the coffee-hounds but certainly could not be camouflaged to look like anything from the pioneer period. During the emigrations, although there were dozens, sometimes hundreds of wagons in a given caravan, each family, or agreed group of people, did their own meal planning and preparation so there was no need for a 40-gallon coffee urn.

There were no fees charged for participating in this adventure, but tickets had been procured by everyone to cover costs of the meals.

The supper time and overnight campout was to be as authentic as reasonable plans could make it. Accordingly, BLM Rangers were posted to deflect visitors who stumbled upon the unmarked trail that led to the location where the night's rendezvous was happening.

During "nooning," there were many who plopped down for a quick nap, and other naps occurred in the evening on full bellies of buffalo stew, beans, fried bread and black coffee. The still, evening air was broken by a squeaky fiddle here, a Jews harp solo there, and guitars. A senior gentlemen, dressed in buckskin, pushed and pulled on an antique concertina. An elderly gentle woman, who was dressed in a wrist-length lace blouse and long black skirt, punished an antique cornet that had nearly all of the original gold finish worn to where the brass shown through. She blew with an obviously well trained but retired embouchure, "The Last Rose of Summer" and "Tenting on the Old Camp Ground."

There was little organized activity other than the outdoor supper. In the background, modern day 2-person and a few 4-person tents were being set up. There were many single and double sleeping bags on ground cloths among the sage. In some wagons, beds were spread—this being a 1-night trip so most wagons were not loaded with all the family belongings on the way to new home in Oregon as would have been the case, say in 1853. Some folks, true to the old trail tradition, unrolled their blankets (modern sleeping bags) on the ground beneath their wagons.

But there were some "chores" to be done. A true pioneer demonstrated the nightly cleaning of his various weapons (he did not carry any bullets on this trip). A pioneer woman was hand sewing a deerskin coat. A smiling lady made a little pot of coffee on a small antique-looking covered stove (that was powered by bottled propane).

As the "walkers," whose feet were now rested and their bodies fortified with buffalo stew, walked among the about two dozen wagons, they admired the authenticity of it all. Antique farm implements were carried on the outsides of wagons. There were wooden barrels

Trail walkers were in costumes of the times. On one wagon was a crate of chickens and a rooster that reminded everyone in the camp that he was there by crowing at all hours of the night.

Interior of a covered wagon. Every item the pioneer family wanted in their new home in Oregon had to he hauled 2,000 miles in the wagon. Wagons were so full there was no place to sleep so the family spread their blankets on the ground under the wagon.

for carrying drinking water. Tied to the back end of one wagon was a hand-made wicker crate containing some live chickens and a rooster. (Every one in camp would, long before dawn, know about that rooster for during the night, as Jim Evans reported later, for no apparent reason at all the bird crowed time and again!)

Come morning, sleeping sacks rolled and tents struck, and the corporate breakfast out of the way, the 1992 wagon train headed west on the last 8-mile stretch for Flagstaff Hill. On arrival at the crossroads there were cheers from the onlookers who had assembled with the horse trailers, campers, and air conditioned automobiles to take the participants on their various ways.

When there are hundreds of people with a common goal, even in a relatively unmanaged but friendly group, everyone assumes his own responsibility. The details and logistics for preparing for this 1992 trail experience had been substantial and the event itself was reported to have been relatively free of miscalculations and mishaps. There were some singed fingers around the cooking fires. There was at least one undeleted expletive when a cup of hot coffee was upset down a guy's shirtfront.

During the evening there was a wild rustle of professional photographers who grabbed madly for their heavy tripoded cameras and backed away in a scurry when, during a so-called "tame," and "controlled" set up, a pair of oxen they were trying to photograph became unruly. The over-burdened photographers were much too close for safety. The oxen, reported to have been somewhat unruly all day on the trail, decided against posing—tried to rear up, "hee'd" and "haw'd" in opposite directions, were doing their best to not be under the control of the teamster who held the reins. The teamster did, for a minute or so, indeed have his hands full.* A large audience had gathered and enjoyed this unexpected action.

Oxen That Would Not Behave

---

*The author was equipped for on-the-spot newspaper-type photography and was not burdened by heavy equipment so could get in then get out quickly. A few pictures from our sequence of this "almost a tragedy" are included here. These were made with an Olympus OM-1 camera with G filter on TMY ASA 400 film at 250th sec.

The only serious accident seems to have been when a rider was bucked off a horse during the day and was hurt. A radio call brought the needed help.

Plausibly the luckiest man on the trip was the gent from Boise who was wearing some antique spectacles. These he had pocketed in his shirt and in some manner they had fallen out. All those horses and people walked over them before the gent missed the glasses. He was not just concerned, he was in a near-frenzy as he had borrowed these priceless glasses just for the day. He and friends went back along the trail making a cautious but frantic search. They found the glasses in the trail. Not a foot of horse or ox or person had stomped them. The glasses were in A-1 condition save for the ever-present dust of the Old Oregon Trail.

Appendix A
Ezra Meeker's Life
Historical Chronology

December 29, 1830	Born near Huntsville, Ohio
1839	Moved to Indiana
May 13, 1851	Married Eliza Jane Summer
April—October 1852	Traversed the Oregon Trail with his wife and 7-week-old son, Marion and brother, Oliver. Arrived in Portland, Oregon Octyober 1, 1852. Moved to Kalama, Washngton where he had his first homestead.
1853—1861	Explored part of Puget Sound with Olliver in small boat. Settled and farmed on McNeill Island, operated a store with Oliver and his father at Steilacoom. Oliver dies while on store buying trip. Expored Fern Hill, now part of Tacoma. Served on jury at trial of Chief Leschi (voted for acquittal).
1862	Moved to Puyallup Valley
1865	Started hop farming, industry with brother John and father.
1877	Platted Puyallup city, at that time named "Franklin."
1885	Beginning of failure of hop farming due to Black aphids (lice).

1887	Construction of Meeker Mansion started.
December 16, 1889	Family moved into the mansion
1890	Mansion completed. Becomes first mayor of Puyallup on incorporation of town August 19, 1890
1892	Reelected Mayor
1893	Financial panic, bank failures, low hop prices, total failure of hop industry.
1896-1901	Went to Yukon gold districts to sell produce from Pacific Northwest. Forms mining company with son, Fred, who died there of pneumonia. Ezra returns to Puyallup to start writing.
1901	Meekers' celebrate Golden Wedding Anniversary at the Mansion.
1903	Researches for book *Pioneer Reminiscences of Puget Sound.*
1906	Begins first trip to retrace Oregon Trail and to promote a transcontinental highway
1909	Eliza Jane Meeker, 75, dies in Seattle at home of daughter Carrie (Mrs. Eban Osborne).
1911	Vacates Mansion due to excessive maintenance required which he could not provide. Mansion became Puyallup House, then home for GAR widows (1915), was nursing home 1948—1968
1928	Ezra Meeker, 97, dies in Frye Hotel, Seattle following visit with Henry Ford in Michigan where Ford was designing a Model A Ford with a covered wagon top for Meeker's next cross-country trip Mr. and Mrs. Meeker buried in Woodbine Cemetery, Puyallup
1970	Ezra Meeker Historical Society, (Inc.) acquires Meeker Mansion for Society's home.

Appendix B
The Meeker Mansion

The Meeker Mansion was deigned by architects Farrell and Darmer, Tacoma. The construction was completed in 1890 during the so-called "Age of Excellence." The tile, marble and interior wood was imported from Europe. Limited data suggests the stained glass

(Top) **Meeker Mansion, Puyallup,** is owned and occupied by the Ezra Meeker Historical Society.

windows were from Povey Studio, Portland, Oregon. Meeker called his home "a pretentious house." He was 32 years old when he arrived in Puyallup and 60 when he took up residence in the mansion.

In 1911 Meeker liquidated his belongings and left the mansion. The house was vacant, except for caretakers for one year.

In 1912 his daughter, Carrie and her husband, Eban Osborne, presented the mansion to the City of Puyallup for use as a hospital. After this use it was returned to the Osborne's. It was vacant, except for caretakers for two years.

The Osbornes sold the mansion to the Grand Army of the Republic (GAR) in 1915 for use as a home for war widows of the Civil War.

In 1948 the mansion was acquired by Dr. Emery King, who use it as a private nursing home.

Dr. King presented the house to the Ezra Meeker Historical Society in 1969 which has operated it to the present time. The Society offers guided tours through the mansion during summer months.

Appendix C
Children of Ezra and Eliza Jane Meeker

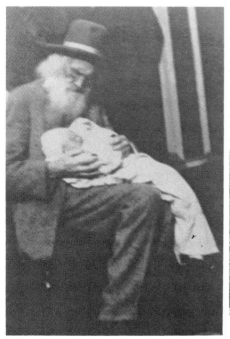 

Ezra Meeker with grandson Wilfred MacDonald in 1899. MacDonald (right) in 1987, displays leather baby shoes worn by his father, Marion Meeker, the first child of Ezra and Eliza Jane.

Marion	Wife: Mary
Ella	Mrs. W. A. Templeton
Thomas	Died in infancy, buried at Steilacoom
Carrie	Mrs. Eban Osborne
Fred	Wife: Clara. Fred buried in Alaska
Olive	Mrs. Roderick MacDonald, buried in B.C.

According to a summery in the Washington State Historical Society, at the time Ezra died he left 15 grandchildren, 20 great-grandchildren plus the descendants of his brother John's family.

Statue of Ezra Meeker in Pioneer Park, Puyallup, Washington.

Appendix D
Ezra Meeker,
Personal Monuments

Ezra Meeker had donated to the City of Puyallup the property now known as Pioneer Park. The Puyallup Ladies Club placed a pergola in the park to mark the site of Meeker's early cabin. Over it was placed ivy which Meeker had brought from England. This was ivy that had originally been planted between the two cabins of his first home in the Puyallup Valley.

The ladies had a stone tablet inscribed "Site of Ezra Meeker's Cabin Home" and placed it in the park. Meeker, at the time of the dedication, was in Elm Creek, Nebraska and he could not attend the dedication. But he recorded a short speech on a phonograph record and this was played in the park during the dedication ceremony. The crowd was so large that all couldn't hear the phonograph so the latter part of the speech was read. The part on the recording was:

This is Ezra Meeker talking June 8, 1912 Elm Creek, Nebraska, 211 miles west of Omaha. I am on my way home to the Pacific Coast. This is my fourth trip with an ox team on the Oregon trail. I crossed the Missouri River 10 miles below Kanesville, now Council Bluffs, Iowa, and drove out from the river on my first trip, May 19, 1852, and arrived at the straggling village of Portland, Oregon October 1 of the same year.

MEEKER

EZRA	ELIZA JANE
BORN	BORN
DEC. 29, 1830	OCT. 15, 1834
DIED	DIED
DEC. 3, 1928	OCT. 8, 1909

Ezra Meeker toward the end of his life. (Lower) Monument for Mr. and Mrs. Meeker, Puyallup's most famous couple.

Appendix E
Meeker Monuments Along the Oregon Trail and Elsewhere

I. Monuments Installed By Ezra Meeker

1.	Tenino Washington	February 21, 1906
2.	The Dalles, Oregon	March 12, 1906
3	Pendleton, Oregon	March 31, 1906
4	Meacham, Oregon	April 5, 1906
5.	LaGrande, Oregon	April 11, 1906
6.	Ladd's Canyon, Oregon	April 11, 1906
7.	Baker City, Oregon	April 19, 1906
8.	Old Mount Pleasant, Oregon	April 21, 1906
9.	Durkee, Oregon	April 1906
10.	Huntington, Oregon	April 1906
11.	Vale, Oregon	April 30, 1906
12.	Fort Boise, Idaho	May 1906
13.	Boise, Idaho	May 9, 1906
14.	American Falls, Idaho	May 1906
15.	South Pass, Wyoming	June 24 1906
16.	Independence Rock, Wyoming	July 3 1906

II. Markers Towns Would Complete (Arranged during 1906 trip)
1. Tumwater, Washington
2. Centralia, Washington
3. Chehalis, Washington
4. Claquato, Washington
5. Jackson Prairie, Washington
6. Toledo, Washington
7. Parma, Idaho
8. Twin Falls, Idaho
9. Pocatello, Idaho
10. Soda Springs, Idaho
11. Montpelier, Idaho
12. Cokeville, Wyoming
13. Casper, Wyoming
14. Glen Rock, Wyoming

15. Douglas, Wyoming
16. North Platte, Nebraska
17. Gothenburg, Nebraska
18. Grand Island, Nebraska

III. Other Markers Suggested to Have Been of Meeker Origin or Instigation
1. Junction of Oregon/California Trail (Idaho: Site not determined)
2. Five miles SW of Scottsbluff, Nebraska (Site not determined)
3. Sun Ranch, Wyoming
4. Burnt Ranch Monument (Site not determined)
5. Fort Hall, Idaho
6. South Pass (1916) (Site not determined)

Appendix F
Miss Clara, Meeker's Trail Cook

When this book was in final process of completion, the authors stumbled on to some unique data. While Meeker and his driver, William Mardon, were on the 1906 venture, they pulled in late one night to the only hotel in Gloversville, New York. Clara Miner worked there but had retired for the night. When the men complained they had not had supper and wished to eat, Clara got up and prepared a hot meal for them.

She and Mardon hit it off well and decided to marry one week later. She joined the team as the cook. "I did all the cooking on the trips we made and Mr. Meeker surely did like my cooking." Clara Mardon left Meeker's employ after about ten years and settled in Bridgeport, Connecticut. She divorced Mardon in 1921 and married Edward Hoover of Bridgeport in 1925.

She reported that since quitting the road with Meeker, she never felt the urge to travel again with few of her neighbors knowing that she once had been greeted by some of the nation's most important personages among them "Teddy" Roosevelt.

About the Authors

Bert and Margie Webber have spent all of their married lives in the Pacific Northwest, and on Margie's side, for two generations before that. Her grandfather, Will E. Hudson, was the first photographer for the *Seattle Post-Intelligencer* and the first newsreel cameraman in the Pacific Northwest. He worked for Pathe´ News and was based in Seattle. Hudson and Ezra Meeker were friends for Meeker was always looking for publicity and Hudson was always looking for a good story. A number of Meeker's early pictures and some of his famous post cards came into Hudson's possession and these have passed through his family to Margie. Some of them are in this book and listed on the Illustration Credits page as "Webber collection."

Bert Webber earned a degree in journalism at Whitworth College as well as a graduate degree in Library Science through Portland State University and the University of Portland. He is the major researcher and writer.

Margie Webber earned a degree in Nursing from the University of Washington and recently retired from a career as a registered professional nurse. She is now an associate researcher and is chief copy editor and proofer. She is also a picture editor and indexer.

Many of the pictures were made by the Webbers in their photolab.

They have four children and at the moment, seven grandchildren. A number of these assist on a time available basis with various phases of operations.

Bibliography

"Bridgeport Woman Tells of Ezra Meeker's Life" in *The Bridgeport [Conn] Herald.* Dec. 9, 1928.

"Covered Wagon Traveler Dies" in *The Bridgeport [Conn.]Times-Star.* Dec. 9, 1928.

Ellison, Robert Spurrier. *Independence Rock; Great Record of the Desert.* Natrona County Historical Society. (Casper, Wyo.) 1930.

Evans, James R., with Bert Webber. *Flagstaff Hill on the National Historic Oregon Trail, Baker City, Oregon—An Interpretive Guide Includes the History of the Pioneer Movement Over the Oregon Trail.* Webb Research Group. 1992.

Ezra Meeker; A Brief Resumé of His Life and Adventures. The Ezra Meeker Historical Society. (Puyallup, Wash.) 1972.

Franzwa, Gregory. *Maps of the Oregon Trail.* Patrice. 1990.

_____. *The Oregon Trail Revisited.* (3rd Ed.) Patrice. 1983.

Gallagher, John S. and Alan H. Patera. *Wyoming Post Offices 1850-1980.* Depot. 1980.

Green, Frank L. *Ezra Meeker–Pioneer; A Guide to the Ezra Meeker Papers in the Library of the Washington State Historical Society.* Washington State Historical Society. 1969.

Hafen, LeRoy R. and Francis M. Young. *Fort Laramie and the Pageant of the West, 1830-1890.* Bison. 1984.

Meeker, Ezra. *The Ox Team on the Old Oregon Trail 1852, 1906.* (Private print) 1906.

_____. *Seventy Years of Progress in Washington.* (Private print). 1921.

Meeker, Scott Cantwell. *Early Wings Over the Trail.* (Private print) 1989.

Nebraska, A Guide to the Cornhusker State. [American Guide Series] Nebraska State Historical Society. 1939.

"The Story of Ezra Meeker" in *The Puyallup Press.* Sept. 22. 1939.

Webber, Bert. *Indians Along the Oregon Trail; The Tribes of Nebraska, Wyoming, Idaho, Oregon and Washington Identified.* (Encyclopedic) Webb Research Group. 1992.

_____. *The Oregon & California Trail Diary of Jane Gould in 1862.* Webb Research Group. 1987.

_____. *The Oregon Trail Memorial Half-Dollar 1926-1939.* Webb Research Group. 1986.

Illustration Credits

Index

Page numbers in *italic* are illustrations
monu = monument